A PO HISTORY OF THE 1916 RISING

THE STORY OF IRELAND'S INDEPENDENCE

Gill Books
Hume Avenue, Park West, Dublin 12

www.gillbooks.ie

Gill Books is an imprint of M.H. Gill & Co.

Copyright © Teapot Press Ltd 2015

ISBN: 978-0-7171-6930-6

This book was created and produced by Teapot Press Ltd

Edited by Fiona Biggs & Ruth Mahony
Designed by Alyssa Peacock & Tony Potter
Illustrated by Bob Moulder & Anthony Morris

Printed in Europe

This book is typeset in Dax, Minion and Albertus

A CIP catalogue record for this book is available
from the British Library.

10 9 8 7

A POCKET HISTORY OF THE

1916 RISING

THE STORY OF IRELAND'S INDEPENDENCE

TARA GALLAGHER, FIONA BIGGS & FIONNBARRA O DUIBHIR

Gill Books

Contents

Introduction 8

The Build-up to 1916:
Home Rule and the Spectre
of the Great Famine

1798: The United Irishmen
Rebellion 10

1800: Abolishing the Irish
Parliament at Dublin 14

1803: Robert Emmet's
Rebellion 16

1829: Daniel O'Connell and
Catholic Emancipation 20

1840: Overturning the Act of
Union of 1800 24

1845–9: *An Gorta Mór* 26

1848 onwards: The Fenians
and the Irish Republican
Brotherhood (IRB) 30

1870: The First Home Rule
Movement Begins 32

1870–82: The Land Acts and
the Land War 34

1912: The Third Home Rule Bill ... 36

1912: The Ulster Covenant
Pledges Unionist Resistance
to Home Rule 40

1913: The Dublin Lockout ... 44

1913: The Founding of the Irish
Citizen Army 48

1880s–1916: Cultural
Nationalism in the Lead-up to
the Rising 50

World War I: The 'War to End
All Wars' 54

1915: The Funeral of Jeremiah
O'Donovan Rossa 58

1915: The IRB Military Council
Plans the Rising 61

The 1916 Rising:
A Chronology

Good Friday 21 April: The Capture
of the German Ship *Aud* 64

Good Friday 21 April: Roger
Casement Arrested 68

Good Friday 21 April: The British
Get Word of the Rising 72

Saturday 22 April: The Countermanding of the Assembly for the Rising — 74

Easter Sunday 23 April: Original Date of the Rising — 78

Easter Monday 24 April: Volunteers Take Over Dublin — 80

Easter Monday 24 April: The Irish Republic is Proclaimed at the GPO — 84

Easter Monday 24 April: Dublin Castle and City Hall — 90

Easter Monday 24 April: St Stephen's Green Occupied — 94

Tuesday 25 April: British Troops Deployed from the Curragh — 98

Tuesday April 25: The World's First Radio Broadcast — 102

Wednesday 26 April: The Rising in Wexford — 106

Wednesday 26 April: The Arrival of the Gun Boat Helga — 108

Wednesday 26 April: British Reinforcements Land at Kingstown — 110

Wednesday 26 April: North King Street Area and Ned Daly — 114

Wednesday 26 April: Sackville Street Shelled — 118

Thursday 27 April: Jacob's Biscuit Factory — 122

Thursday 27 April: Boland's Mill Shootout — 126

24–29 April: The Rising in Galway — 130

Thursday 28 April: Cathal Brugha Wounded at the South Dublin Union — 132

Friday 28 April: The Rising in Ashbourne — 136

Friday 28 April: The GPO Abandoned — 140

Friday 28 April: Clery's Department Store and the Imperial Hotel on Sackville Street Collapse — 142

Friday 28 April: General Maxwell and the Imposition of Martial Law — 144

Friday 28 April: Last Stand on Moore Street **146**

Saturday 29 April: The Volunteer Leaders Surrender **150**

3 May–3 August: The Executions and Their Consequences **154**

Reactions of the Irish General Public **160**

Reactions of the British General Public **164**

The Aftermath of the 1916 Rising and the Birth of Modern Ireland

1919: The Emergence of Sinn Féin **166**

1919: The First Dáil Meets **170**

1919: The War of Independence Begins **174**

1920: The Act for the Partition of Ireland Passed **178**

1921: The Anglo-Irish Treaty Signed **182**

1922: The Death of Michael Collins **186**

1922: The Irish Free State is Established **190**

1930s: Fianna Fáil and Éamon de Valera **194**

1937: The Constitution of Ireland **198**

1973: Ireland Joins the EEC **202**

1970s: Northern Ireland and the Troubles **206**

1998: The Good Friday Agreement **210**

2010s: Modern Ireland **214**

Biographies

Michael Collins **220**

James Connolly **222**

James Craig **224**

Éamon de Valera **226**

William Gladstone **228**

Maud Gonne **230**

Arthur Griffith **232**

James Larkin **234**

David Lloyd George **236**

Constance Markievicz **238**

Séan O'Casey   **240**
Daniel O'Connell   **242**
Charles Stewart Parnell   **244**
Pádraig Pearse   **248**
John Redmond   **250**
W.B. Yeats   **252**

Credits   **254**

Introduction

Though short, the events of the 1916 Rising cast a long shadow over the subsequent Irish fight for independence and the birth of the modern nation.

Full of stories of one of Ireland's best known historical events, this pocket history recalls the country's struggle for independence, as epitomised by the bloody battle of the 1916 Rising. The Rising was an armed insurrection in Ireland during Easter Week 1916, mounted by Irish republicans to end British rule in Ireland and establish an independent Irish Republic while the United Kingdom was preoccupied with the events of World War I.

Organised by seven members of the Military Council of the Irish Republican Brotherhood (IRB), the six-day rebellion was the culmination of a long history of rebellion in the Irish quest for independence, which is explored in this book. *A Pocket History of the 1916 Rising* is an insightful condensed guide to what is arguably the most important event in the history of the Irish nation, providing information on the background to the 1916 Rising, a blow-by-blow account of the short and bloody revolt, its consequences and its continuing reverberations a century later.

1798: The United Irishmen Rebellion

The 1798 rebellion, one of the bloodiest rebellions ever to take place in Irish history, had its roots in the deep discontent of the Catholic majority with the political and social inequalities that were rife in Ireland at the time.

In the late 18th century, most land, wealth and political power in Ireland was held by a handful of the population, the Protestant ascendancy, Anglo-Irish land-owning families that had settled in Ireland in the wake of the English conquest during the 16th century. The Catholic population was deeply disadvantaged by the Penal Laws, which excluded Catholics from ownership of land, education and, at a time when the electoral franchise was extended only to landowners, the vote. Punitive measures controlling trading in goods from Ireland were only finally relaxed in the late 1930s.

As a consequence, Catholic emancipation (the blanket term applied to the drive to free Catholics from these disadvantages) was one of the hot political issues of the time. The majority of the ascendancy opposed Catholic emancipation, fearing the loss of their many advantages and the attendant possibility that Ireland would detach itself from British rule. Ironically, however, many of those who campaigned and fought for Catholic emancipation had been born into the ascendancy.

In the late 18th century, Ireland did not have full legislative freedom – laws passed by the Irish parliament could be ratified only with the consent of the British parliament at Westminster. There were Irish politicians, such as Henry Grattan, who wanted Catholic emancipation without breaking Ireland's tie to England. Theobald Wolfe Tone, a Dublin-born Protestant lawyer, was inspired by the American and French revolutions to found the Society of United Irishmen in 1791 to campaign for parliamentary reform by securing the equality and freedom of all Irishmen of all religions. He declared that the aim of the United

THEOBALD WOLFE TONE
requested a soldier's execution by firing squad and when his request was denied, avoided death by hanging by cutting his throat.

Irishmen should be 'to break the connection with England, the never-failing source of all our political evils'.

Over time the aim of the United Irishmen changed to full independence by armed insurrection, and after an unsuccessful attempt to land a French fleet at Bantry Bay in 1796, Wolfe Tone made plans for an uprising for May 1798.

In Dublin, the planned epicentre of the 1798 rebellion and the location of most of the leaders, the starting signal was to be the halting of the mail coaches into the city. Unfortunately, the authorities were alerted by a spy, and the leaders were arrested less than an hour before the rising was to start. Without leadership, the plans for Dublin were abandoned.

On 24 May the rebellion took place across the rest of the country, but was quickly crushed, except in County Wexford. Under the leadership of Father John Murphy, a band of rebels took the towns of Enniscorthy and Wexford before suffering devastating defeats in the next few battles and regrouping to lick their wounds at Vinegar Hill, outside Enniscorthy.

Meanwhile, in County Antrim in northern Ulster, the United Irishmen rose in support of Wexford. After this rising was defeated on 10 June (now called 'Pike Sunday'), County Down rebelled. A shopkeeper called Henry Munro led the rebels into battle at Ballynahinch where the fighting raged for two days before the insurgents were defeated with the loss of several hundred men. On 16 June, Munro was hanged and decapitated outside his own front door.

Meanwhile, at Vinegar Hill, 20,000 British soldiers surrounded the rebels. In the end the battle lasted only two hours, with the badly equipped rebels hammered by British artillery, suffering hundreds of casualties. From August 1798, several small bands of French soldiers landed in Mayo and Donegal and had some small victories, but with no significant reinforcements coming from France and the rebellion crushed in the rest of the country, the French surrendered. Wolfe Tone was arrested on a French ship, the *Hoche*, and was taken to Dublin where he was tried for treason and sentenced to death.

THE BATTLE OF VINEGAR HILL
A priest who tries to intercede is shot and killed.

1800: Abolishing the Irish Parliament at Dublin

In 1782 Henry Grattan had been successful in introducing the Constitution of 1782, which gave the Irish parliament the independence to control its own agenda and legislate for Ireland. It was later known as Grattan's Parliament.

HENRY GRATTAN was in favour of Catholic emancipation and wanted to reform the Irish parliament to allow it to make laws independently, although he was loyal to Britain.

Grattan's Parliament was doomed after the devastation of 1798. The British government, led by Prime Minister William Pitt, was alarmed by the lack of political stability in Ireland. Britain was in a vulnerable position, having lost its American colony in the American War of Independence (1775–83), and with the continuing war between Britain and France, it became expedient to strengthen links between Ireland and England.

Lord Cornwallis, as commander-in-chief of the British army, had put down the 1798 rebellion, and Pitt now appointed him Lord Lieutenant of Ireland in order to help guide the Act of Union through the Irish parliament (it had to be passed in the British parliament and the Irish parliament).

The Act of Union reversed the autonomy of Grattan's Parliament, and was underpinned by the belief that the 1798 rebellion had been provoked by the frustration of the Catholic population at Protestant misrule as well as the strictures still imposed on them and capitalised on by the United Irishmen. Lord Cornwallis, working with Lord Castlereagh and supported by Pitt, indicated that Catholic emancipation would be an absolute a priority after the Union, quickly gaining the support of the Catholic population.

LORD CORNWALLIS was another casualty of the failure to deliver Catholic emancipation when he resigned as Lord Lieutenant.

The Protestant Irish parliament remained hostile to the idea of the union and to Catholic emancipation, but inducements were offered to gain their support, and in March 1800 the Irish parliament agreed to the terms of the Act of Union.

Though Pitt had every intention of introducing the promised reforms on Catholic emancipation, King George III refused to support him and Pitt resigned.

1803: Robert Emmet's Rebellion

After the failure of the 1798 rebellion, a young Trinity College student, Robert Emmet, reorganised the United Irishmen and began to plan another rebellion.

Emmet was influenced by the leaders of the 1798 rebellion, in particular Wolfe Tone. From 1800 to 1802 he lived in Europe with United Irishmen veterans of 1798. While there, Emmet secured French support for an insurrection and began to prepare for the French landing on his return to Ireland. However, the authorities were alerted to the United Irishmen plot when, in July 1803, an explosion at Emmet's arms depot made him decide to bring the rebellion forward.

Emmet likely knew the rebellion would be a dismal failure – his compatriot Thomas Russell had had little luck raising any support in Ulster and the promised French invasion had failed to materialise – yet he insisted the rising go ahead.

Emmet's rebellion began badly, and got worse. Various factions of the rebels either failed to receive or failed to heed the call to arms. Only 80 of the 2,000 rebels Emmet had expected arrived at their meeting point in Dublin, and many of those who did turn up were drunk. A clash with police on Thomas Street turned into a riot, and Lord Kilwarden, a Dublin judge, was pulled from his carriage and piked to death. Kilwarden had argued for clemency for Wolfe Tone during his trial, but was widely hated for his sentencing of another United Irishman, William Orr, to death.

MURDER OF LORD KILWARDEN

An engraving by George Cruikshank (1792–1878).

Emmet went into hiding as the authorities searched for the leaders of the rebellion, and was captured when he unwisely moved his hiding place to be near his

sweetheart, Sarah Curran. He was tried, sentenced to death and on 20 September in Dublin he was hanged and beheaded on Thomas Street. A memorial to him still stands on Thomas Street today.

Emmet achieved the status of a martyr after his death, due in part to his bravery (or foolhardiness) in proceeding with the rebellion when he knew it would most likely fail, and in part because of his stirring speech from the dock, worthy of the accomplished orator that he was:

'Let no man write my epitaph: for as no man who knows my motives dare now vindicate them, let not prejudice or ignorance asperse them. Let them and me repose in obscurity and peace, and my tomb remain uninscribed, until other times, and other men, can do justice to my character; when my country takes her place among the nations of the earth, then, and not till then, let my epitaph be written. I have done.'

IRISH NATIONALIST ROBERT EMMET (1778–1803)
Execution of Robert Emmet, in Thomas Street, 20 September 1803. *Most Irishmen look idly on, while England assassinates at will!* Print by J. Kirwan.

O'CONNELL MONUMENT
by John Hentry Foley stands at the top of O'Connell Street in Dublin.

1829: Daniel O'Connell and Catholic Emancipation

In 1823 Daniel O'Connell, a Catholic-born lawyer, founded the Catholic Association, an organisation that would spearhead the campaign for Catholic emancipation.

O'Connell abhorred the violence of the 1798 and 1803 rebellions and it was his intention to achieve home rule in a peaceful manner, through Catholic emancipation. O'Connell was a highly accomplished public speaker and strategist; although the Catholic Association membership came initially from the middle-class elite with an annual subscription equivalent to what an average farmer would pay for six months' rent, within a year associate members were encouraged to join at a penny a week – the so-called 'Catholic rent'. This move swelled the ranks of the association, providing O'Connell with the exact number of his supporters with which to leverage the British government. It also succeeded in politicising the wider Catholic population.

In 1825, alarmed by the rapid spread of the organisation and its involvement with the Catholic Church, the British government passed an act outlawing it, a move that was neatly side-stepped by O'Connell, who dissolved the association and established a new one that conformed to the letter of the new legislation.

There was some support for Catholic emancipation in the ranks of the House of Commons, but King George IV's absolute opposition to the idea meant that earlier attempts to legislate for it had failed to pass through the House of Lords. To strengthen support in the Commons, O'Connell encouraged Irish voters to elect only pro-emancipation candidates, rather than their local landlords as was the accepted practice, and had some success. Many of those who voted against their landlords paid the price when they were evicted from their homes. From 1828 the

DANIEL O'CONNELL proposing the formation of the Catholic Association, 1825.

campaign accelerated. O'Connell stood for election in County Clare, despite the fact that he would not be able to take his seat in the House of Commons if he won – as a Catholic, he could not take the Oath of Supremacy, which was an oath of loyalty to the British monarch as Supreme Governor of the Church of England.

This put the Prime Minister – Arthur Wellesley, the Duke of Wellington – and Home Secretary Robert Peel in a quandary; they could either push through a Catholic Emancipation Act and let O'Connell take his seat or be forced to declare the election invalid and risk open revolt in Ireland. Public sympathy for Catholics in England was high at that time and Wellington and Peel wanted to avoid bloodshed in Ireland.

After much wrangling, in the Roman Catholic Relief Act became law in April 1829 and O'Connell was thereafter known as the Liberator. Catholics now had the right to vote and to be members of parliament in the British or Irish parliaments. However, the new act also contained a key provision to which O'Connell had had to agree – the minimum property qualification for voters was to be increased to five times its value, meaning that most Catholics still would not qualify.

DANIEL O'CONNELL
portrayed in a 19th-century engraving.

1840: Overturning the Act of Union of 1800

O'Connell's next aim was to repeal the Act of Union to achieve home rule, which would allow Irish Catholics and Protestants to govern themselves in a Dublin parliament independent of Britain, but loyal to the British monarch. He founded the Repeal Association in 1830 to achieve this.

GREEN PROTEST
As it was illegal for anyone to bear green flags or political banners at public demonstrations, thousands held green boughs, bushes and even trees, so the meeting processions resembled 'walking forests'.

O' Connell initiated a series of mass peaceful gatherings called 'monster meetings', where hundreds of thousands of people gathered. The first, in Trim in March 1843, attracted 30,000 people, while the May meeting in Cork was attended by up to half a million. These meetings were intended to send a clear message of strength to Sir Robert Peel, now the British Prime Minister, who was vehemently opposed to home rule.

The largest monster meeting of all was set for Sunday 8 October 1843 at Clontarf, the historic battleground where the great King Brian Boru had fallen, but on the evening of 7 October Peel banned the meeting, bringing in armed cavalry to Clontarf and positioning two naval vessels in Dublin Bay to further dissuade the organisers of the meeting. O'Connell feared a bloodbath if the meeting went ahead and called it off, encouraging the public to respect the ban. Despite this, O'Connell was arrested and sentenced to a year in jail in London, though this was overturned and he was released after three months.

In his later years O'Connell met resistance within the home rule movement from a group called Young Ireland. The Young Irelanders were a group of young Repeal Association members associated with *The Nation*, a newspaper founded at Trinity College, committed to uniting all Irishmen to a nationalist cause regardless of religion. Originally great admirers of O'Connell's work, over time his refusal to countenance violence as a means to independence led the Young Irelanders to abandon his party and split from the Repeal movement.

THE NATION was a nationalist newspaper published in the 19th century, founded by two Catholics, Charles Gavan Duffy and Thomas Davis, and a Protestant, John Blake Dillon.

1845–9: *An Gorta Mór*

The Great Famine was a disaster made ten times worse than it might have been by the effects of British policy in Ireland in the years preceding the outbreak of the famine, coupled with a woefully inadequate response by the British government of the time to the unfolding crisis.

NATIONAL FAMINE memorial designed by Irish artist John Behan, which portrays a coffin ship full of dying people.

One disastrous piece of policy that contributed to the scale of the disaster was the Penal Law of 1704. This provided that any land bequeathed by a Catholic had to be divided between his sons, both illegitimate and legitimate, meaning that by the 1840s vast numbers of families farmed minuscule plots of land.

Since its introduction into Ireland in the 16th century the potato, originally used a supplementary

THE POTATO BLIGHT

The harvest first failed in 1845, with potato plants across Ireland affected by the potato blight, a fungus called *phytophthora infestans* that thrived in the mild and wet Irish climate. The potato plants appeared healthy from above, but once dug up the tubers began to disintegrate into rotten slush within days or hours of harvesting.

food, had become very popular due to its abundant, nutritious cropping and ease of cultivation in what were often small plots of land with poor soil. The average daily male consumption in the 18th century was 4.5–5.5 kg/10–12 lb.

With enough food and a time of relative peace after the 1798 rebellion, the Irish population had exploded to around 8.5 million by 1846, the first year the potato crop failed, with about 4 million – almost half the population – depending on the potato as their staple food.

A potato disease that ravaged Europe in the 1840s caused widespread failure of the potato crop in Ireland. With some 40 per cent of the population subsisting on potatoes, this caused mass starvation and disease. This period is sometimes referred to as the Irish Potato Famine, but often in Ireland as the Great Hunger or *an Gorta Mór*.

In 1846, 60 per cent of the population lived in meagre huts of sod and turf and many rented their land. This contributed to the scale

A FAMILY struggle to find potatoes that are not affected by blight. The potato was a staple food in many Irish people's diet.

of the devastation – forced evictions were common as landlords took the opportunity to remove poverty-stricken farmers and labourers from their land and replace them with paying tenants. The number of evictions from 1846 to 1854 is estimated to have been more than half a million.

Peel took a practical approach to the famine, setting up relief schemes so that labourers could earn the money necessary to purchase food, though wages were still pitifully low. He decided against banning the export of Irish-produced food – a source of some bitterness to the Irish, who were starving in a country that was abundant in dairy and grain – to avoid angering the landowners who were achieving good prices abroad.

Peel did, however, provide a measure of relief, allowing the import and distribution of 'Indian corn' from the United States, sold at cost price.

The famine might not have taken such a disastrous toll had Peel not been replaced as Prime Minister in 1846 by the Whig party leader John Russell. Though Russell himself was sympathetic to the dire situation of the Irish poor, Sir Charles Trevelyan, a man of pious morals, was placed in charge of the relief schemes. He described the famine as an 'effective mechanism for reducing surplus population', a 'judgement of God' on the Irish peasants for their Catholicism and idleness.

Thus Trevelyan's relief schemes were harsh – a very effective soup kitchen scheme, which, at the peak of its operation, fed three million people a day, was dismantled after only six months in 1847, the most devastating year of the Great Hunger, yet deemed the last year of the famine by the government. The workhouses, already overburdened with the starving and fever-ridden, required hard physical labour from people to earn their relief. 1847 also brought a cruel amendment to the Poor Law – no family with more than a quarter of an acre of land could receive relief. This was a calculated move to force smallholders from their tiny patches of land, rendering them destitute and homeless.

The human cost of the famine was incalculable, but the numbers give some scale: at least 1 million of the population died of starvation or famine-related disease such as cholera and typhoid, and 1 million emigrated. One of the cruellest and most futile initiatives occurred in 1847, after the potato crop had failed twice. Relief committees tasked the starving with building famine roads for pay so low it was almost worthless – the roads led nowhere, stopping abruptly when most of the workers had died, exhausted.

CONDITIONS IN THE WORKHOUSES
were extremely grim, with families requried to work hard for relief.

1848 onwards: The Fenians and the Irish Republican Brotherhood (IRB)

The period after the famine was marked by a series of revolutions across Europe, with 1848 dubbed 'The Year of Revolutions'. Inspired by these, in 1848 about 100 Young Irelanders, led by James Stephens among others, rose up to attack police in Ballingarry, County Tipperary.

JAMES STEPHENS
Founder of the Irish Republican Brotherhood.

The rising led to an ignominious defeat in a domestic garden, which soon became known as the Battle of Widow McCormack's Patch, and the insurgents were sentenced to transportation to Australia. James Stephens was rescued from jail and escaped to Paris, where he dedicated himself to learning the basics of revolution. After his return to Ireland in 1856 he founded the IRB (the Irish Republican Brotherhood, or the Irish Revolutionary Brotherhood – it was never clear which word the 'R' stood for), a secret organisation dedicated to achieving independence through armed insurrection.

A year later in New York a sister society known as the Fenians was founded. Membership of both organisations swelled and all became known as Fenians.

The IRB suffered from disorganisation and was infiltrated by many spies, so when, in March 1867, a lukewarm rebellion took place in Munster and Dublin, it was swiftly put down and the insurgents transported to Australia.

A GROUP OF MEN
surrounding a bonfire on a mountaintop during an IRB insurrection in Tipperary.

THE MANCHESTER MARTYRS

Fenianism might have died with this lacklustre revolution, but for the Manchester Martyrs. In September 1867 a group of Fenians attempted the rescue of a Fenian prisoner from the back of a police van and, in shooting the lock off the door, fatally injured Sergeant Charles Brett who was escorting the prisoner. The three Fenians who were tried, William Allen, Michael Larkin and Michael O'Brien, were convicted of murder and condemned to death. The three became martyrs. Irish nationalist feeling was galvanised by the harshness of their punishment – no Irish rebel had suffered capital punishment for nearly 70 years – and by their stirring Robert Emmet-esque speeches from the dock.

1870: The First Home Rule Movement Begins

In May 1870, Isaac Butt founded the Home Government Association, later known as the Home Rule League. It was a parliamentary party whose aim was the achievement of self-government for Ireland within the British Empire.

GLADSTONE'S AIM
Upon becoming Prime Minister, William Gladstone stated 'My mission is to pacify Ireland'.

A conservative Protestant educated at Trinity College, Butt was a member of parliament who, despite his earlier disparagement of Daniel O'Connell, had become a critic of British mismanagement of Ireland and had defended many Fenians in his capacity as a lawyer.

William Gladstone, Prime Minister of Britain from 1868 to 1874 and leader of the Liberal Party, was critical of the violent methods of the Fenians, but was also committed to rectifying the injustices of British rule in Ireland. At the time, the privileged position of the Church of Ireland was a bone of contention with the Irish public. This 'national' church had a membership that represented a tiny fraction of the population, but the whole population, Catholic and Protestant, had to pay 'tithes' or duties to the church, which owned vast amounts of property. In 1869 Gladstone dismantled these powers, then turned his attention to the Irish dissatisfaction with the landlord–tenant system.

WILLIAM GLADSTONE

at the despatch box in the British Houses of Parliament.

PARNELL
Monument at the
junction of O'Connell
and Parnell Streets,
Dublin.

1870–82: The Land Acts and the Land War

William Gladstone's Land Act of 1870 was intended to give more security to tenants, forbidding exorbitant (or 'rack') rents, providing for 'security of tenure' and the chance to buy their holding if the landlord agreed to sell.

In practice the Act was counter-productive. Most landlords did not wish to sell their land, few peasants could afford to buy, and disputes over what constituted 'rack' rents worsened relations.

After Isaac Butt's death in 1879, the Home Rule League, now known as the Irish Parliamentary Party, elected Charles Stewart Parnell as its leader. An Anglo-Irish landowner and nationalist, Parnell felt there was a natural connection between the 'land campaign' and the campaign for home rule.

In 1879, as a result of mounting evictions due to an economic downturn, the Land League was founded by Michael Davitt, a former IRB member, to campaign for more rights for small tenant farmers. Later that year Parnell became its president. The struggle between small tenant farmers and landlords, led by Parnell and the Land League, became known as the Land War, which fought for the introduction of the 'Three Fs' – fair rent, fixture of tenancy and freedom to sell.

The Land League's methods were peaceful. Parnell ordered members to shun anyone who moved into a farm from which the previous farmer had been evicted, any landlord who charged rack rents and evicted tenants, and any shop or other business that traded with those shunned. This initiative was the origin of the term 'boycott', which entered the lexicon when a landlord's agent, Charles Boycott, was shunned by the local community in 1880.

In 1881 Gladstone attempted to bring a conclusion to the Land War with the Land Act, which made fair rents a matter of law, but the Land League refused to accept it. After a particularly incendiary speech, Parnell was arrested and spent six months in prison, until an agreement on the Land Act was reached with Gladstone. The Land War had been won.

MICHAEL DAVITT was an Irish republican and an agrarian agitator. He founded the Irish National Land League.

1912: The Third Home Rule Bill

KITTY O'SHEA, as she was known to her enemies (Katie to her friends), had a long-running relationship with Charles Stewart Parnell, eventually causing his downfall.

After campaigning for years for tenant rights, Parnell turned his attention to home rule. He joined Isaac Butt's Home Rule League in 1874, and became its leader in1880. He increased the power of the party, boosting its membership numbers and efficiency.

In response to over ten years of campaigning from Parnell's Home Rule League, later renamed the Irish Parliamentary Party, Gladstone introduced the Government of Ireland Bill in 1886 – the first Home Rule Bill. Gladstone had been committed throughout his years in power to achieving peace in Ireland and he believed that creating a devolved parliament would achieve this. However, Gladstone's bill was defeated by his own MPs. When Parnell became embroiled in scandal, named as co-respondent in the divorce case of his mistress, Kitty O'Shea, his reputation collapsed and the Irish Parliamentary

Party split, with most abandoning him. Two years later he was dead.

In 1893 Prime Minister Gladstone introduced a second Home Rule Bill, getting it through the Commons, only to see it roundly rejected by the House of Lords. However, feelings on the question of Irish home rule were softening.

After Parnell's death, John Redmond took over the leadership of the Irish Parliamentary Party and, with his low-key but steady leadership, successfully steered it back to unity and the pursuit of home rule.

In 1910 a parliamentary reshuffle brought about a change in the balance of power in the British parliament that left Redmond holding more cards than ever before. Taking advantage of this, he was instrumental in bringing about the abolition of the House of Lords' veto, so that they could no longer reject laws passed by the House of Commons – merely delay their enactment by two years. Redmond persuaded the Liberal government of Prime Minister Asquith to introduce the third Home Rule Bill in 1912.

CHARLES STEWART PARNELL
depicted on a cigarette card. He was described by Gladstone as the most remarkable person he had ever met. He was a nationalist and land reformer.

CONSTANCE MARKIEVICZ
was a Sinn Féin and Fianna Fáil politician, revolutionary and suffragette.

The bill was hugely contentious – the new generation of Irish nationalists was vehemently opposed to the bill, viewing its moderate progression towards self-government through political channels as weak, and little more than toadying to a foreign power. Numbered among this new breed of nationalists were many of the key players in the 1916 Rising, including the 50-year-old Fenian Tom Clarke, Bulmer Hobson, Constance Markievicz, Pádraig Pearse and Seán MacDermott.

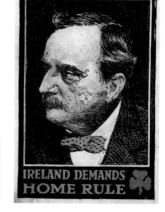

JOHN REDMOND
portrayed on a rare home rule label from 1912.

IRELAND DEMANDS HOME RULE

PÁDRAIG PEARSE

TOM CLARKE

SEÁN MACDERMOTT

BULMER HOBSON

1912: The Ulster Covenant Pledges Unionist Resistance to Home Rule

NEWSPAPER
advertisement
looking for rifles.

In 1912 tensions surrounding the third Home Rule Bill were running high. Nationalist factions were split into moderates, like John Redmond, who believed the best way forward was to achieve home rule gradually through concessions from the British government.

On the other side were the republicans, including Tom Clarke and Pádraig Pearse, who believed home rule was too little, too late. They embraced violent revolution as the only means to achieving an independent Irish republic. In 1912 Ireland was rapidly becoming a polarised and militarised society – and nowhere more so than in Ulster.

In September 1912, in response to the third Home Rule Bill, more than 250,000 unionists signed the Ulster Solemn League and Covenant by which they pledged before God never to accept home rule.

Their reasons for objection to the bill were more than understandable – Ulster's population was largely Protestant and it was fearful that home rule would eventually lead to an independent, Catholic Ireland, which would contravene their own wish to stay part of the British and Irish Union and loyal to the Crown. Fears that the policies of a Dublin parliament might also favour the Catholic south, penalising vital industries in the north, such as ship-building and linen milling, were also rampant.

A SILLY GAME
Sir Edward Carson: 'ULSTER WILL FIGHT!' Mr Punch: 'WHAT! AGAINST FREE SPEECH? THEN ULSTER WILL BE *WRONG!*'

The Covenant was not a risk in itself, but the situation became potentially dangerous when the Ulster Volunteer Force (UVF) was founded by Edward Carson in 1912. The UVF soon numbered 90,000 and represented a militarisation of Protestant opinion. Its purpose was to block home rule for

Ireland by military means. Starting out without arms or organisation, the UVF soon became a force to be reckoned with, gathering stocks of arms and bullets purchased in Germany, which made their way onshore in April 1914.

In response, the 160,000-strong nationalist Irish Volunteers also made moves to arm themselves. The Irish Volunteers included members of nationalist organisations such as the Gaelic League, Ancient Order of Hibernians, Sinn Féin and the IRB.

FIGHTERS
in the UVF were well armed, with munitions bought from Germany.

A NORTHERN POWDER KEG

The third Home Rule Bill exposed long-running tensions between Protestant and Catholic interests in Northern Ireland. Against a background of much wrangling and under the threat of war provoked by the UVF's arms importation, the Home Rule Bill was ultimately reworked so that the six heavily Protestant counties in Ulster – Antrim, Down, Armagh, Fermanagh, Tyrone and Londonderry – would be permanently partitioned from Ireland, and would stay under the rule of Britain.

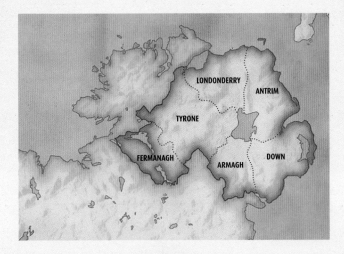

1913: The Dublin Lockout

The living conditions of the urban working class in Dublin were largely ignored by nationalists until 1913. It was a modern problem, caused by increasing industrialisation in Ireland, which drew large quantities of unskilled people to the cities in search of work.

JAMES CONNOLLY
was a revolutionary socialist and trade union leader, born in Edinburgh of Irish parents.

In 1913, wages in Dublin were barely half of those in London and a third of the population lived in tumbledown tenements without running water or toilets. Three-quarters of the workforce was unskilled and a fifth was unemployed.

James Connolly was an Irish republican and socialist labour leader who had grown up in extreme poverty in an Irish area of Edinburgh. In 1896, after the birth of his third daughter, he moved his family to Dublin to take up work with the Dublin Socialist Society. He believed that there was a connection between Irish independence and workers' rights.

Frustrated that socialist ideas had not yet taken hold sufficiently in Ireland to bear fruit, he left for the United States in 1903, returning in 1910 to become right hand man to James Larkin, a docker's union official.

In 1908, Larkin had been sent to Dublin to recruit members, but realising the extent of the need for labour organisation in Ireland, he stayed in Dublin, founding the Irish Transport and General Workers' Union (ITGWU) that same year. The union exploded in popularity, building to a membership of 10,000 by 1913. The union embraced Larkin's socialist principles, workers' rights and an independent Ireland.

JAMES LARKIN rousing the crowd with one of his speeches.

The response from business-owners was negative – in 1911 foundrymen in Wexford had been 'locked out' of their jobs by their employers for joining the union, and a year later union members were expelled from the workforce at the Belfast shipyards.

In August 1913, Larkin decided to break the anti-union stance of the Dublin United Tramway Company (DUTC). This was a daunting undertaking, as the DUTC was owned, along with the *Irish Catholic* and other Irish nationalist newspapers and the city's largest department store, by William Martin Murphy, a former Irish Parliamentary Party MP and a nationalist. Murphy demanded that all employees reject membership of the ITGWU or be fired, and in response Larkin staged a walk-out. Murphy was as good as his word and locked the workers out, so Larkin orchestrated further strikes at businesses that supported Murphy.

At its peak the dispute involved 20,000 workers and 80,000 of their dependants, who, as time went on with no pay and no strike benefits, began to suffer starvation. Employer-sponsored violence was also rife, from both the police and the Ancient Order of Hibernians (a Catholic organisation along the lines of the Orange Order), and picket lines soon turned into battlegrounds.

By January 1914, starving and weak, the workers had lost the dispute, and in October, frustrated at the outcome, Larkin left for the United States. He might have lost the Dublin Lockout, but he left behind him a politicised workforce who retained strength in numbers.

A PROCLAMATION

WHEREAS it has been represented to me, being a Justice of the Peace in and for the County of the City of Dublin by an information duly sworn, that a number of persons will meet or assemble at

SACKVILLE STREET
OR ITS NEIGHBOURHOOD

in the said County of the City of Dublin, on or about

the 31st day of AUGUST, 1913

and that the object of such Meeting or Assemblage is seditious, and that the said Meeting or Assemblage would cause terror and alarm to, and dissension between, His Majesty's subjects, and would be an unlawful assembly.

NOW I do hereby prohibit such Meeting or Assemblage, and do strictly caution and forewarn all Persons whomsoever that they do abstain from taking part in or encouraging or inciting to the same.

AND I do hereby give notice that if in defiance of this Proclamation any such Meeting or Assemblage at Sackville Street or its neighbourhood shall be attempted or take place, the same will be prevented and all Persons attempting to take part in or encouraging the same, or inciting thereto, will be proceeded against according to law.

AND I do hereby enjoin all Magistrates and Officers intrusted with the preservation of the Public Peace, and all others whom it may concern, to aid and assist in the due and proper execution of the Law in preventing any such Meeting or Assemblage as aforesaid, and in the effectual dispersion and suppression of the same, and in the detection and prosecution of those who after this Notice, shall offend in the respects aforesaid.

Given under my hand this 29th day of August, 1913.

E. G. SWIFTE,
Chief Divisional Magistrate, Dublin Metropolitan Police District.

GOD SAVE THE KING.

1913

PROCLAMATION issued by E.G. Swift, Magistrate of the Dublin Metropolitan Police District, in an attempt to stop the huge public meeting that Larkin had called for, planned to take place on Sackville Street on Sunday 31 August 1913. Larkin publicly burned the proclamation.

1913: The Founding of the Irish Citizen Army

JAMES CONNOLLY had British military experience in his youth, which he put to great use, saying that the ICA should 'drill and train as they were doing in Ulster'.

James Connolly, socialist labour leader and Larkin's right-hand man during the Dublin Lockout, founded the Irish Citizen Army (ICA), a small well-trained militia of four battalions of trained men in November 1913.

The ICA's initial purpose was to enable the locked-out workers to defend themselves and to protect them from the police during the often-violent demonstrations.

After Larkin left Ireland in 1914, James Connolly took command of the ICA and the organisation became a more revolutionary one dedicated to the creation of an Irish republic. General Secretary Seán O'Casey, who later became one of Ireland's most celebrated dramatists, provided a constitution that declared that 'the ownership of Ireland, moral and material, is vested by right in the people of Ireland'. Other prominent early members included Constance Markievicz, Francis Sheehy-Skeffington and P. T. Daly.

Connolly believed that achieving independence through an armed rebellion in the tradition of the Fenians was legitimate, and the organisation lost members when a proposal to allow dual membership of the much larger Irish Volunteers was not passed. More members left when Connolly's sympathies with the IRB became clear, and by 1916 the organisation's membership had been reduced to about 200 to 300.

Speech from the Dock

By F. SHEEHY SKEFFINGTON

The Occasion of his Trial under the Defence of the Realm Act, in the Dublin Police Court in June, 1915

"A Magnificent Defence of Free Speech"

FRANCIS SHEEHY-SKEFFINGTON
was a prominent pacifist. He was murdered by Captain J.C. Bowen-Colthurst in 1916.

PRE-EMPTIVE ACTION

A small number of IRB members within the Irish Volunteers movement had started to plan a rising. Worried that Connolly would embark on premature military action with the ICA, they approached Connolly and inducted him into the IRB's Supreme Council to co-ordinate their preparations for the armed rebellion that became known as the Easter Rising.

MAURICE DAVIN
(1842–1927) was
an Irish farmer who
became co-founder
of the Gaelic
Athletic Association.
He was also the
first President of
the GAA and the
only man ever to
serve two terms
as its president.

1880s–1916: Cultural Nationalism in the Lead-up to the Rising

At the start of the new century, Ireland was in the grip of change.

The galvanising of political feeling by the Home Rule Bill, the rise of militant socialist and nationalist groups, and a renewed interest in Gaelic culture meant that cultural nationalism – which defines a 'nation' by its shared culture – had fertile soil in which to grow.

The Great Famine had proved to be a watershed for Ireland, changing the country irrevocably. There was good and bad to this – literacy, social mobility and transport networks across the country improved, but the proportion of those for whom Irish was their mother tongue plummeted, with the number of *gaelgóirs* falling from 23 per cent in 1851 to a mere 14 per cent in 1901.

This led to concerns among nationalists that the unique Irish identity was in danger of being anglicised out of existence. In 1884 the Gaelic Athletic Association (GAA) was founded by a teacher, Michael Cusack, to promote the playing of traditional Irish games, such as hurling and Gaelic football, and to discourage the spread of 'foreign' games, such as soccer and rugby. From its inception the GAA was an openly nationalist organisation, even banning membership to anyone who watched or played 'foreign' games and any members of the British army or the police.

In 1893, less than ten years later, the Gaelic League (Conradh na Gaeilge) was founded by Eoin MacNeill and Douglas Hyde to encourage Irish culture through the teaching of the Irish language and activities such as Irish dancing, music and poetry. By 1904 the League had 593 branches and 50,000 members. Though not explicitly a political group, it attracted those who were politically minded, often Anglo-Irish, like Maud Gonne and Douglas Hyde, both of whom had learned Irish as adults.

MAUD GONNE was an English-born Irish revolutionary, actress and suffragette. She had a turbulent relationship with the poet W.B. Yeats.

ABBEY THEATRE, DUBLIN,
programme cover.

The Irish literary revival was another example of cultural nationalism. It included poets, writers and playwrights who took inspiration from Irish folklore and popular culture. It was dominated by writers from Anglo-Irish backgrounds such as W.B. Yeats who were sympathetic to independence. The movement established a national theatre, the Abbey Theatre, in 1904 to produce Irish drama.

By celebrating Ireland's unique culture, these movements indirectly called into question Britain's right to control Ireland, by challenging the effects Britain's culture was having on Ireland. To preserve its unique identity, in the eyes of these organisations Ireland must achieve complete separation from Britain. The IRB capitalised on this and used both the GAA

W.B. YEATS was a driving force behind the Irish literary revival and was one of the founding members of the Abbey Theatre.

and the Gaelic League as recruiting grounds – Douglas Hyde quit the League in 1915 owing to its large membership of IRB men.

A NEW LEASE OF LIFE FOR THE IRB

In 1905 Denis McCullough and Bulmer Hobson set out to revitalise the flagging IRB with the aim of achieving an independent Irish Republic. By 1914 the IRB's Supreme Council was dominated by those committed to a violent uprising, including Bulmer Hobson, Denis McCullough, Patrick McCartan, John MacBride, Michael (The) O'Rahilly, Pádraig Pearse, Seán MacDermott and Tom Clarke. MacDermott and Clarke were to be the primary instigators of the Easter Rising in 1916; The O'Rahilly was shot by British troops during the final hours of the Rising in a lane off Moore Street, Dublin.

World War I: The 'War to End All Wars'

With the outbreak of World War I in August 1914, the British government agreed that the implementation of home rule would be put on hold until the war was over.

DIVIDED LOYALTY
The 1916 Rising did not have much public support in Ireland because large numbers of Irishmen had volunteered for the British army to fight in the Great War.

In the north of Ireland, Edward Carson, the founder of the Protestant Ulster Volunteers and first signatory to the Ulster Covenant, volunteered the UVF to fight in the British army. In the south, in the interests of unity, John Redmond also pledged his largely Catholic Irish Volunteers to the fight.

This caused a bitter split in the Irish Volunteers – some 105,000 were loyal to Redmond and enlisted to fight in the war with Britain, becoming known as the National Volunteers. The remaining 12,000 members kept the

name Irish Volunteers under the leadership of Eoin MacNeill, a professor of early Irish history at University College Dublin. The position of the Irish Volunteers was that Ireland should remain neutral. They were opposed to an uprising against the British government except in the case of a crisis – for example, the forced conscription of Irishmen into the British army or any attempt by Britain to disband the Irish Volunteers.

INFILTRATION

The IRB was prepared to use violent revolution to achieve independence, and thus they were a secret society. Eoin MacNeill, leader of the Irish Volunteers, did not support them, but some of the key positions of the Irish Volunteers had over time been co-opted by high-level IRB conspirators, including Pádraig Pearse, Tom Clarke, Joseph Plunkett and Thomas MacDonagh.

JOHN REDMOND, pictured with his wife and probably his daughter, around 1914. He was leader of the Irish Parliamentary Party from 1908 to 1918.

For Redmond's Irish Parliamentary Party, the best outcome would be that the war between England, France and Germany would be a short one and that after victory was declared and the National Volunteers

STAINED-GLASS windows in the Guildhall, Derry, commemorating the Irish Divisions who served in WWI.

had demonstrated their loyalty and been honoured for their service, home rule would be conceded and Ireland would become an independently ruled member of the British Empire, alongside Australia and Canada.

The Ulster Volunteer Force and the National Volunteers fought bravely in the war. The 36th (Ulster) Division was made up almost entirely of men from the UVF and fought in the opening offensive in the Somme in France – in their first two days' action they lost 5,000 men. The National Volunteers fought in the 10th Division, with over 9,000 killed or wounded, and in the 16th (Irish) Division, who were practically wiped out; at one point they fought side-by-side with their Ulster Volunteer counterparts.

IS **YOUR** HOME WORTH FIGHTING FOR?

IT WILL BE TOO LATE TO FIGHT WHEN THE ENEMY IS AT YOUR DOOR SO JOIN TO-DAY

WWI POSTER
From 1915 and printed in Dublin, encouraging men to sign up to fight in WWI.

1915: The Funeral of Jeremiah O'Donovan Rossa

The funeral of Cork-born Fenian Jeremiah O'Donovan Rossa on 1 August 1915 was a spark that further fanned the flame of Irish revolutionary feeling.

O'Donovan Rossa was a long-time revolutionary and member of the Fenians and had spent years serving a life sentence for his part in agitating towards a rising in the 1850s. Freed under the 1870 Fenian Amnesty act,

he was released on condition that he would never again return to Ireland. Exiled, he migrated to New York where he was active in Clan na Gael, the American branch of the IRB.

O'Donovan Rossa was arguably the most famous of all Fenian leaders throughout Ireland and, sensing an opportunity, Tom Clarke, co-leader of a secret group inside the

IRB (itself a secret organisation) that was planning an uprising, requested that O'Donovan Rossa's body be returned home for burial. O'Donovan Rossa's funeral was expertly stage-managed by Clarke and his co-conspirator Seán MacDermott as an unofficial state funeral – the largest the country had seen in living memory. His body was returned to Ireland from New York and taken to Glasnevin cemetery, followed by a procession of Irish Volunteers in full dress uniform and thousands of ordinary citizens.

At the graveside, the Irish Volunteers gave a 21-gun salute and Pádraig Pearse, a senior Irish Volunteer, poet, writer, and secret IRB conspirator, gave a speech designed to inflame the revolutionary feelings of every Irish Volunteer and able-bodied man in attendance, casting the Irish Volunteers as the natural successors of the Fenians and closing with the famous words:

THE O'DONOVAN ROSSA MEMORIAL in St Stephen's Green in Dublin, Ireland.

'The Defenders of this Realm have worked well in secret and in the open. They think that they have pacified Ireland. They think that they have purchased half of us and intimidated the other half. They think that they have foreseen everything. They think that they have provided against everything; but the fools, the fools, the fools! — they have left us our Fenian dead, and while Ireland holds these graves, Ireland unfree shall never be at peace.'

Recruited into the IRB in 1913, Pearse had come to the leaders' attention for his oratory – MacDermott had recommended Pearse to Clarke for his verbal skill, saying 'if you give him the lines he will dress it up in beautiful language,' and it was this skill that led to Pearse being asked give the speech at O'Donovan Rossa's funeral.

1915: The IRB Military Council Plans the Rising

In August 1915 the IRB Military Council was formed and began to plan the uprising in earnest.

The two main planners of the Rising, Tom Clarke and Seán MacDermott, feared the very thing that John Redmond and the Irish Parliamentary Party wanted – a swift end to World War I, and with it the slipping away of the opportunity for revolution.

By 1915 the IRB were getting restless and increasingly worried that the public demands of James Connolly for a rising supported by his 200-strong ICA would alert the British government to their own plot. After an Irish Volunteer meeting at which Connolly spoke frankly about his intentions, Pearse, himself a conspirator from the Military Council of the IRB, assured Eoin MacNeill, the leader of the Irish Volunteers, that he could convince Connolly to desist. He alerted the IRB Military Council, who collected

EOIN MACNEILL photographed in 1913.

THE DRIVING FORCE BEHIND THE RISING

Though the Military Council of the IRB had seven members – Tom Clarke, Seán MacDermott, Pádraig Pearse, Éamonn Ceannt, Joseph Plunkett, James Connolly and Thomas MacDonagh – the driving force of the inner core were Clarke and MacDermott. Clarke had been sentenced to penal servitude for life for his part in the Fenian bombing campaign in London in the 1880s. His sufferings in prison marked him for life – in his fifties he was a fierce-eyed, stooped, bearded and seemingly old man. Following his return to Ireland after a government amnesty, Clarke ran a tobacconist on Parnell Street that he used as his base of political operations. In 1908 the much younger Seán MacDermott, son of a Leitrim farmer, met Clarke, forging a relationship that was central to the 1916 Rising. MacDermott was a charismatic, silver-tongued character who believed wholeheartedly in the necessity of violent sacrifice to achieve independence.

Connolly from Liberty Hall in Dublin, and, after three days of negotiation, swore him onto the Military Council of the IRB.

The IRB Military Council eventually comprised seven members: Tom Clarke, Seán MacDermott, Pádraig Pearse, Éamonn Ceannt, Joseph Plunkett, Thomas MacDonagh and Connolly. The plan of the Military Council to mount an armed rebellion led by IRB men, supported by the Irish Volunteers (which had been infiltrated by the IRB), and to fight with arms landed in the west of Ireland by German forces excited Connolly, who only had the backing of his 200 ICA men. The planned rising was to take place on Good Friday, 21 April 1916, centred on an insurrection in Dublin and supported by arms and troops from Germany, which would be landed in Kerry.

SEÁN MACDERMOTT photographed before 1916.

A MONTAGE OF THE LEADERS of the 1916 Rising executed by the British. Tom Clarke is seated in the centre and Seán MacDermott is to his right shoulder.

Good Friday 21 April: The Capture of the German Ship *Aud*

Sir Roger Casement, an officer in the British Foreign Service, was an unusual addition to the IRB Military Council.

An idealist opposed to colonial exploitation, he had successfully fought British exploitation in Africa, and was committed to a German–Irish alliance that would liberate Ireland. In his IRB capacity he travelled to Germany in 1914 to convince the German establishment to support Irish independence and provide not just arms, but a whole force to invade and drive out the British. Unfortunately, Casement proved the wrong man for the job; the Germans regarded him with bemusement, and his pet project of recruiting an Irish brigade made up of Irish prisoners of war to lead the charge achieved the recruitment of only 56 men.

The IRB Military Council sent reinforcements to Casement in the form of Joseph Plunkett, the sensitive, highly educated son of a papal count. Plunkett was terminally ill with tuberculosis and, on the pretext of travelling for a cure, he joined Casement in Germany to collaborate on a document called the Ireland Report, which detailed how Germany could launch an Irish–German military campaign, in effect joining Ireland with the Central Powers fighting against the Allies in the World War I. The Germans said they would review the plans. Plunkett went home, while Casement remained in Germany.

JOSPEPH PLUNKETT contracted tuberculosis at an early age. He was a founder of the Irish Esperanto League and a member of the Gaelic League.

With the date of the Rising set for Good Friday, 21 April 1916, the IRB asked the German military for a submarine to support the Rising from Dublin Bay, field artillery, senior officers to lead the rank and file, and arms and ammunition. The planned arrival date of the ship was 19 April. However, the date of the Rising was changed to Easter Sunday, 23 April, and so the rebels

AUD-NORGE

THE GERMAN SHIP SS *LIBAU*, also known as the SS *Castro*, was renamed the *Aud* and disguised as a Norwegian fishing vessel.

requested the German military to delay the ship until that date.

The IRB Military Council and the German military could communicate only through messages passed by German diplomats and Clan na Gael, an Irish republican organisation in the United States, and so the German ship *Aud*, which had no radio, was already en route to Ireland disguised as a Norwegian fishing vessel to avoid detection when the message came to delay its arrival.

The IRB Military Council was unaware that the British had cracked German codes earlier in the year and knew the true identity of the *Aud*. Anchoring off Fenit in Kerry on 21 April, the *Aud* waited in vain for the local Irish Volunteers to respond to their signals, but the rebels were not expecting the ship for another two days and were unaware of its early arrival. After some anxious waiting, the ship was pursued by British vessels until the captain scuttled the ship along with its contents of 20,000 rifles, ammunition and explosives. The Germans had provided no artillery, submarine or senior officers to lead the charge in a rebellion of which they knew very little.

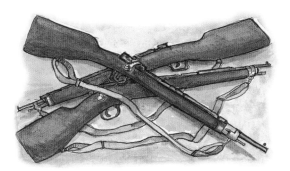

THE *AUD*
had an estimated million rounds of ammunition on board, as well as machine guns and explosives – none of which reached Ireland.

Good Friday 21 April: Roger Casement Arrested

ROGER CASEMENT
painting by Sarah Purser, around 1913. He was arrested and hanged in England at Pentonville Prison in 1916. This picture is at the National Gallery of Ireland.

Meanwhile, Casement's relations with the Germans had deteriorated to the extent that he learned only by accident of the planned Easter Rising and the proposed German assistance – which was much less than had been requested, and much less than Casement had hoped for.

Believing that the Rising was doomed with such a small, token shipment of arms and worried that the Germans would not support the Irish rebels and would instead use the Rising for their own gain, Casement claimed he had to go to Ireland to meet the arms shipment. A submarine was provided to take him and two others, Daniel Bailey and Robert Monteith, to the arranged rendezvous point with the *Aud*. The *Aud* was not at the rendezvous but was anchored some miles away out

A DIPLOMAT TURNED NATIONALIST

Roger Casement grew up in County Antrim. He joined the British Foreign Office, where he had a successful diplomatic career. He created two important consular reports, one on the exploitation of the Belgian Congo by Leopold II, King of the Belgians, and the other on atrocities carried out by a British rubber manufacturing company against the Putamayo Indians in Peru. This work against injustice earned him a knighthood in 1911. It was his passion for challenging colonial abuse that led to his involvement with the Irish nationalists.

of sight, and after some deliberation the trio left the submarine in a dinghy and headed for the shore.

After reaching the shore near Ardfert, the dinghy containing the three men capsized on Banna Strand. Casement was ill and too weak to run, so he urged his companions to escape. He took refuge in McKenna's Fort while Bailey and Monteith tried to make contact with the local IRB. Casement was arrested by suspicious British police. As the opening salvos of the Easter Rising were fired, Casement found himself in the Tower of London awaiting trial for treason, espionage and sabotage.

ROGER CASEMENT
travelled to Ireland
from Germany by
submarine.

Casement was tried and convicted of treason and sentenced to death. His address from the dock is regarded as one of the greatest speeches of all time:

'Self-government is our right, a thing born in us at birth; a thing no more to be doled out to us or withheld from us by another people than the right to life itself – than the right to feel the sun, or smell the flowers or to love our kind. It is only from the convict these things are withheld, for crime committed and proven – and Ireland, that has wronged no man, that has injured no land, that has sought no dominion over others – Ireland is being treated today among the nations of the world as if she were a convicted criminal.

'If it be treason to fight against such an unnatural fate as this, then I am proud to be a rebel, and shall cling to my 'rebellion' with the last drop of my blood. If there be no right of rebellion against the state of things that no savage tribe would endure without resistance, then I am sure that it is better for men to fight and die without right than to live in such a state of right as this. Where all your rights have become only an accumulated wrong; where men must beg with bated breath for leave to subsist in their own land, to think their own thoughts, to sing their own songs, to gather the fruits of their own labours – and even while they beg, to see things inexorably withdrawn from them – then surely it is a braver, a saner and truer thing to be a rebel, in act and in deed, against such circumstances as these than to tamely accept it, as the natural lot of men.'

Casement was hanged at Pentonville Prison in London on 3 August 1916, at the age of 51.

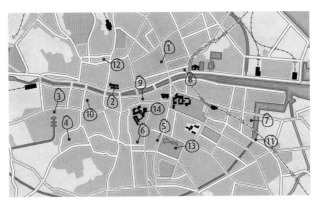

MAIN SITES

1. General Post Office (GPO)
2. The Four Courts
3. South Dublin Union
4. Jameson's Distillery
5. The Royal College of Surgeons

6. Jacob's Biscuit Factory
7. Boland's Mill
8. Liberty Hall
9. City Hall
10. Mendicity Institute

11. Mount Street Bridge
12. North King Street
13. St Stephen's Green
14. Dublin Castle

THEN AND NOW

Some of the names of the streets and buildings have changed since the Rising in 1916. Others no longer exist. Liberty Hall (8) was left in ruins after the Rising and, despite restoration, it was demolished in the 1950s and replaced by a new building. Sackville Street in the city centre is now O'Connell Street. The South Dublin Union (3) is now St James's Hospital. Jacob's Biscuit Factory (6) is now the Dublin Institute of Technology.

Good Friday 21 April: The British Get Word of the Rising

It may seem strange that the British authorities did not act to put down the Rising as soon as they had learned about Casement's plans for a German arms shipment.

British military intelligence was aware that the Irish revolutionary element was planning some sort of action. The Chief Secretary for Ireland, Augustine Birrell, and the Under Secretary, Matthew Nathan, were of the opinion that, in the long run, some form of autonomous Irish rule was coming and that an attempt to suppress Irish military groups such as the Irish Volunteers would be needlessly antagonistic. Although they could easily have put down the badly armed, half-trained men, this might have led to a full-scale revolution, which was precisely what they wished to avoid. It was for this reason that a mock insurrection on St Patrick's Day, when Irish Volunteers 'attacked' Dublin Castle, was ignored by the authorities.

On the other hand, Lord Wimbourne, the Lord Lieutenant of Ireland, believed that these military groups must be disarmed – a view shared by British military intelligence.

Over Easter Birrell went to London to attend a Cabinet meeting, leaving things in the hands of Under Secretary Nathan, who believed that after the capture of Roger Casement – assumed to be masterminding the rebellion – and the scuttling of the *Aud*, there was no way that a rising would still go ahead. Nonetheless, on Easter Saturday Wimbourne argued for full-scale arrests, but Nathan refused without Birrell's agreement. This request did not reach Birrell in time and on Monday morning the 1916 Rising started.

MATTHEW NATHAN was a British soldier and colonial administrator. Birrell and Nathan's careers were effectively ended by the Rising – they both resigned.

Saturday 22 April: The Countermanding of the Assembly for the Rising

BULMER HOBSON
meeting James
McGarrity around
1900.

The official head of the IRB was Bulmer Hobson. He had originally been a close friend of Tom Clarke, until they split with much bitterness after Hobson, albeit reluctantly, gave John Redmond, leader of the Home Rule Party, control over the Irish Volunteers.

Hobson believed that otherwise the Irish Volunteers would split and the organisation would collapse. Clarke refused to forgive him for it, which explains why, although Hobson was the ostensible leader of the IRB, its Military Council kept their plans for an uprising secret from him.

Eoin MacNeill, leader of the Irish Volunteers, was also kept in the dark, as he was committed to the Irish Volunteers not taking part in any rebellion unless they were under threat from British military suppression. The vast majority of the Volunteers would not rise without his orders.

The Military Council's way around Eoin MacNeill was to circulate a document, known as the Castle Document, which appeared to lay out Dublin Castle's intentions to strike pre-emptively against many Irish nationalist organisations, including the Irish Volunteers. Whether the document was a real

MEN OF THE WEST
(detail © DACS) by Seán Keating shows the painter and two images of his brother Joe. Joe was a member of the Irish Volunteers and possibly the IRB.

contingency plan, taken from Dublin Castle and embellished by James Connolly to convince MacNeill to strike, or a total forgery, its effect was just what the Military Council had hoped for. MacNeill put the Irish Volunteers on alert, psychologically preparing them for battle as they watched for any sign of a threat.

On Thursday 20 April, MacNeill learned of the conspiracy from Hobson, who had himself been tipped off only after a suspicious Volunteer commander had questioned orders he had received from Pearse to alert Volunteer companies around the country to rise on Easter Sunday, 23 April. They were to parade in full kit and this was to be the signal for the Rising to begin. Hobson and MacNeill immediately confronted Pearse at St Enda's, the school he ran in Dublin, getting him out of bed. A furious MacNeill gave Hobson authority to countermand the orders and went home to bed. Upon waking on Friday morning, Hobson decided to wait until Saturday to issue the countermanding orders, a ploy to prevent Pearse having enough time to intercept them. However, that morning, Seán MacDermott went to see MacNeill and convinced him that the Rising was inevitable and that countermanding the orders would only cause confusion, taking advantage of MacNeill's belief that the Castle Document was genuine and that the British might strike at any moment against the Volunteers and impose military rule in Ireland.

MacNeill acquiesced, to Hobson's disgust, and on Good Friday it seemed the rebellion would go ahead on Easter Sunday. Hobson was kidnapped and held by the IRB, who were intent on keeping him out of the way, which MacNeill seemed to accept. However, on Easter Saturday, all changed utterly.

BULMER HOBSON
was kidnapped at gunpoint and held at a safe house in Phibsborough to keep him out of the way until the Rising was well under way.

Easter Sunday 23 April: Original Date of the Rising

Three loyal members of the Irish Volunteers came to Eoin MacNeill on Saturday afternoon with information that threw his conversation with Seán MacDermott and his agreement to support the Rising into an entirely different light.

EOIN MACNEILL in a pensive studio photograph.

They shared the news that the *Aud* had been scuttled, her precious arms lost and Roger Casement arrested – something that the IRB Military Council had kept from MacNeill – and, another blow, that the Castle Document was a forgery.

MacNeill was horrified; catastrophic defeat, bloodshed and the ruin of the Irish Volunteers were now surely the only outcomes of a rebellion, let alone the implications of the lies on which his agreement with MacDermott had been based. Aided by members of the Irish Volunteers loyal to him, including The O'Rahilly, Sean Fitzgibbon and Arthur Griffith, he rapidly wrote orders to the heads of the Irish Volunteer squadrons, cancelling all manoeuvres and marches and making it explicit that there was to be no rising on Sunday. In a stroke of genius, he also sent word to the editor of the *Sunday Independent* that he was coming in person to give an important announcement that must be published in Sunday's paper. At a little after one o'clock in the morning he handed his message to the editor, and the next morning, emblazoned across the paper, was an order reading: *'Owing to the very critical position, all orders given to the Irish Volunteers for tomorrow, Easter Sunday, are hereby rescinded, and no parades, marches, or other movements of Irish Volunteers will take place.'*

The IRB Military Council met the same morning and spoke at length about their options. Outwardly, they decided they would support the new orders, but secretly they would get word to battalions to rise on the Monday instead. The ink was still damp on the Proclamation of the Irish Republic and Pearse was set to become the President of the new republic after the very private Tom Clarke had refused the post.

IRISH VOLUNTEERS
inside the GPO pose
for a photograph.

Easter Monday 24 April: Volunteers Take Over Dublin

LIBERTY HALL
was a hotel before it became the fortress of James Connolly. Maud Gonne and Constance Markievicz had earlier run a soup kitchen here.

Early on Monday morning, preparations were being made at Liberty Hall for mobilisation. At 11:00 a.m., to general surprise, The O'Rahilly showed up with a car full of weapons – since avoiding a rising was now impossible, he felt he had to be part of it and see it through.

Approximately 1,500 Irish Volunteers and ICA members turned out, fewer than would have come had the orders not been countermanded by O'Neill, but enough to hearten those who did take part. At Liberty Hall 400 Irish Volunteers and ICA men gathered under James Connolly, who was de facto acting commander-in-chief of the military forces of the 1916 Rising. Connolly had trained the rebels in the kind of guerrilla warfare they would need to defeat the much better armed and resourced British army – many of whom were Irish themselves, home from the French trenches. The plan was to take various key defensive positions around the city from which to target any British reinforcements, including the General Post Office (GPO), the Four Courts (Dublin's main law court), Jacob's Biscuit Factory, St Stephen's Green, Boland's Mill near Grand Canal Dock and the South Dublin Union (now St James' Hospital).

THE GPO
became the headquarters of the 1916 Rising and site of fierce battles with British forces before it was burnt out as a result of heavy shelling.

On the morning of Easter Monday, 140 rebels, including James Connolly and four more members of the IRB Military Council, Pádraig Pearse, Tom Clarke, Seán MacDermott and Joseph Plunkett, seized the GPO and set up the headquarters of the Rising there.

The Magazine Fort in the Phoenix Park was raided for British military arms and explosives by a task force made up of Irish Volunteers and members of Na Fianna Éireann, a scouting organisation set up in 1909 by Constance Markievicz, Hobson and others. Bombs were set to destroy any contents the rebels had not been able to access. The bombs exploded successfully, but the fort did not contain much in the way of arms, which had been removed to support the war effort.

A Volunteer outpost of 17 men was set up on Mount Street to guard the approach to the city centre

THE SO-CALLED 'Gorgeous Wrecks' stumbled upon a rebel position and four of them were killed in the ensuing fight before fleeing.

from the port at Kingstown (now Dún Laoghaire) where the British were likely to land troops. On Monday a group of reserve forces of the British army, locally nicknamed the 'Gorgeous Wrecks', owing to their age and the motto 'Georgius Rex' on their uniforms, stumbled upon the rebel position. Four of the reserves were killed, while the rest fled to the nearby Beggars Bush Barracks.

A NEW REPUBLIC

The Proclamation of the Irish Republic was almost not ready in time. The printing was begun on Easter Sunday in the basement of Liberty Hall, but had to be halted because there was not enough type available to create the top and bottom at the same time, and so the document was not ready until Monday morning.

Easter Monday 24 April: The Irish Republic is Proclaimed at the GPO

The GPO was chosen as the headquarters for the Rising as it was situated on Dublin's main street, Sackville Street (later renamed O'Connell Street), contained a telegraph office and was high enough for snipers to do their work easily from the roof.

After the initial storming with bayonets, which cleared out most of those inside except the handful of British soldiers taken prisoner, The O'Rahilly took charge of removing from the building its remaining civilians, the clerks and postal workers, which he did calmly and with courtesy. Half an hour after the building was stormed, the new tricolour flag of green, white and orange was run up the flagpole at the Henry Street corner and another with the inscription *IRISH REPUBLIC* in gold on a green background was raised on the Prince's Street side.

At 12:45 p.m. Tom Clarke handed the proclamation to Pádraig Pearse, who walked out in front of the building and, watched by a bemused crowd, declared an Irish Republic and read the proclamation aloud.

Dubliners were at best lukewarm in their reception of the rebels. On Monday evening the Commissioner of the Dublin Metropolitan Police ordered his men off the street after three had been killed – at least one by the ICA forces occupying St Stephen's Green, who remembered their treatment at the hands of the police during the Dublin Lockout in 1913. With the police gone, looting became widespread in the city centre, and the poverty-stricken general population smashed windows and grabbed whatever they could, watched in dismay by the rebels in the GPO.

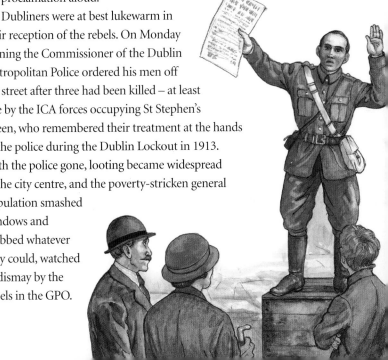

PÁDRAIG PEARSE reading the Proclamation to a surprised crowd.

WALTER OSBORNE
painted studies of the poverty-stricken and dispossessed in Ireland. This painting is at the Hugh Lane Gallery, Dublin.

The first signatory to the proclamation was Tom Clarke, in deference to his seniority and his life-long commitment to Irish independence, for which he had suffered so much. The proclamation had as its central tenets religious and civil freedom and equal rights and opportunities to all its citizens, regardless of creed. Daniel O'Connell would have been proud.

POBLACHT NA H EIREANN.

THE PROVISIONAL GOVERNMENT

OF THE

IRISH REPUBLIC

TO THE PEOPLE OF IRELAND.

IRISHMEN AND IRISHWOMEN : in the name of God and of the dead generations from which she receives her old tradition of nationhood, Ireland, through us, summons her children to her flag and strikes for her freedom.

Having organised and trained her manhood through her secret revolutionary organisation, the Irish Republican Brotherhood, and through her open military organisations, the Irish Volunteers and the Irish Citizen Army, having patiently perfected her discipline, having resolutely waited for the right moment to reveal itself, she now seizes that moment, and, supported by her exiled children in America and by gallant allies in Europe, but relying in the first on her own strength, she strikes in full confidence of victory.

We declare the right of the people of Ireland to the ownership of Ireland, and to the unfettered control of Irish destinies, to be sovereign and indefeasible. The long usurpation of that right by a foreign people and government has not extinguished the right, nor can it ever be extinguished except by the destruction of the Irish people. In every generation the Irish people have asserted their right to national freedom and sovereignty: six times during the past three hundred years they have asserted it in arms. Standing on that fundamental right and again asserting it in arms in the face of the world, we hereby proclaim the Irish Republic as a Sovereign Independent State, and we pledge our lives and the lives of our comrades-in-arms to the cause of its freedom, of its welfare, and of its exaltation among the nations.

The Irish Republic is entitled to, and hereby claims, the allegiance of every Irishman and Irishwoman. The Republic guarantees religious and civil liberty, equal rights and equal opportunities to all its citizens, and declares its resolve to pursue the happiness and prosperity of the whole nation and of all its parts, cherishing all the children of the nation equally, and oblivious of the differences carefully fostered by an alien government, which have divided a minority from the majority in the past.

Until our arms have brought the opportune moment for the establishment of a permanent National Government, representative of the whole people of Ireland and elected by the suffrages of all her men and women, the Provisional Government, hereby constituted, will administer the civil and military affairs of the Republic in trust for the people.

We place the cause of the Irish Republic under the protection of the Most High God, Whose blessing we invoke upon our arms, and we pray that no one who serves that cause will dishonour it by cowardice, inhumanity, or rapine. In this supreme hour the Irish nation must, by its valour and discipline and by the readiness of its children to sacrifice themselves for the common good, prove itself worthy of the august destiny to which it is called.

Signed on behalf of the Provisional Government,

THOMAS J. CLARKE.
SEAN Mac DIARMADA.   THOMAS MacDONAGH.
P. H. PEARSE.   EAMONN CEANNT.
JAMES CONNOLLY.   JOSEPH PLUNKETT.

THE PROCLAMATION was printed in Liberty Hall the day before the Rising. The use of different typefaces is due to a shortage of type as a result police raids on the building. Only around 2,500 copies were run off and they were either left around to be picked up by passers-by or posted up in the nearby streets. A copy of the Proclamation sold at auction in 2008 for €360,000.

IRISHMEN AND IRISHWOMEN: In the name of God and of the dead generations from which she receives her old tradition of nationhood, Ireland, through us, summons her children to her flag and strikes for her freedom.

Having organised and trained her manhood through her secret revolutionary organisation, the Irish Republican Brotherhood, and through her open military organisations, the Irish Volunteers and the Irish Citizen Army, having patiently perfected her discipline, having resolutely waited for the right moment to reveal itself, she now seizes that moment, and supported by her exiled children in America and by gallant allies in Europe, but relying in the first on her own strength, she strikes in full confidence of victory.

We declare the right of the people of Ireland to the ownership of Ireland and to the unfettered control of Irish destinies, to be sovereign and indefeasible. The long usurpation of that right by a foreign people and government has not extinguished the right, nor can it ever be extinguished except by the destruction of the Irish people. In every generation the Irish people have asserted their right to national freedom and sovereignty; six times during the past three hundred years they have asserted it in arms. Standing on that fundamental right and again asserting it in arms in the face of the world, we hereby proclaim the Irish Republic as a Sovereign Independent State, and we pledge our lives and the lives of our comrades in arms to the cause of its freedom, of its welfare, and of its exaltation among the nations.

The Irish Republic is entitled to, and hereby claims, the allegiance of every Irishman and Irishwoman. The Republic guarantees religious and civil liberty, equal rights and equal opportunities to all its citizens, and declares its resolve to pursue the happiness and prosperity of the whole nation and of all its parts, cherishing all of the children of the nation equally, and oblivious of the differences carefully fostered by an alien Government, which have divided a minority from the majority in the past.

Until our arms have brought the opportune moment for the establishment of a permanent National Government, representative of the whole people of Ireland and elected by the suffrages of all her men and women, the Provisional Government, hereby constituted, will administer the civil and military affairs of the Republic in trust for the people.

We place the cause of the Irish Republic under the protection of the Most High God, Whose blessing we invoke upon our arms, and we pray that no one who serves that cause will dishonour it by cowardice, inhumanity, or rapine. In this supreme hour the Irish nation must, by its valour and discipline, and by the readiness of its children to sacrifice themselves for the common good, prove itself worthy of the august destiny to which it is called.

Easter Monday 24 April: Dublin Castle and City Hall

Seán Connolly of the ICA had recently been made captain by James Connolly, and was charged with capturing City Hall as he knew the area well.

SEÁN CONNOLLY
shot and killed Constable James O'Brien, a policeman on duty at Dublin Castle.

First, however, he and his column of 30 men (and about ten women – the ICA was the only nationalist organisation that accepted women as equal members) attempted to capture Dublin Castle. Upon seeing them marching towards the gates, the policeman on duty, a Constable James O'Brien, waved at them to move aside and attempted to close the gates. Connolly shot him in the chest and urged the rest of the company to rush the castle, where the rebels captured and tied up several guards in the guardroom but failed to gain access to the castle itself. Inside was Under Secretary Matthew Nathan, who was waiting for the arrival of a telegram from Chief Secretary Augustine Birrell in London granting the authority for the arrest of the Irish Volunteer leaders.

After the gates of Dublin Castle were closed, Seán Connolly moved his company on to occupy City Hall, where they established themselves on the roof. From there Connolly shouted orders to other rebels on neighbouring roofs and they shot at British troops for some hours before Connolly, failing to crouch sufficiently low as he moved back and forth on the rooftop, was shot and killed by a sniper. The rest of the company, including Seán Connolly's 15-year-old brother Matthew, were demoralised and left rudderless by the loss of their leader and were unable to hold their position. By that

AN ICA MEMBER stands guard with a rifle.

night the British were bombing and machine-gunning the back of City Hall to gain entry. They proceeded through the building floor by floor until the whole garrison was captured. They were confused by the presence of women, initially believing that they must be prisoners of the ICA rather than soldiers in its ranks.

THE BRITISH ARMY brought in machine guns, which the rebels did not have.

The existence of Irish nationalist women's groups such as Cumann na mBan and the egalitarian policies of the ICA meant that there were many female key players in the Rising. Kathleen Lynn was a medical doctor and

an active suffragette and labour activist. After the Rising she established a hospital, St Ultan's Hospital for Infants, with a group of female activists who believed more support was needed for poor women with children. Also on the roof of City Hall with Connolly's party was Helena Molony, a longtime nationalist and labour activist and a close friend of Kathleen Lynn and Constance Markievicz. Markievicz was active in the Irish suffragette movement and the nationalist movement and was a staunch supporter of workers' rights and friend of the poor. She was a very theatrical figure and assumed great visibility during the Rising, due in part to her costume of green riding breeches, tunic, ammunition belt and hat complete with ostrich feather.

KATHLEEN LYNN in a portrait by Lily Williams from the 1920s. When Seán Connolly died, Captain Kathleen Lynn, chief medical officer of the 1916 Rising, took over – it was she who made the surrender to the British at City Hall.

Easter Monday 24 April: St Stephen's Green Occupied

The 22-acre public park may not have been the most practical choice for the rebels to defend – it was bordered on all sides by railings and overlooked by multi-storey buildings – but it had been chosen for its central location and excellent transport links to the rest of the city.

CONSTANCE MARKIEVICZ

posing in a studio with her pistol.

The St Stephen's Green strike was headed by Michael Mallin, James Connolly's trusted second-in-command, an unimposing figure at only five feet seven inches. He had served for years in the British military, before training as a weaver, and had joined the ICA in 1913 after becoming involved in trade union activities.

Initially Mallin, with Markievicz as his second-in-command, took the park with only 36 ICA men and supporting units of women and Fianna, ejecting crowds of surprised civilians who were enjoying a sunny Easter bank holiday in the park. However, as the word got out that MacNeill's countermand had been broken, many joined the garrison there until a total of 104 ICA members were fighting at St Stephen's Green.

A HORSE KILLED in the fighting near St Stephen's Green.

Shortly after the park was secured, an unarmed police constable, Michael Lahiff, was shot dead. Though it is unclear what happened, tensions between the police and the ICA had been high since their violent clashes during the Dublin Lockout in 1913, and it was rumoured that Markievicz was responsible for the shooting.

While the park was secured with trenches and barricades made of passing motor vehicles commandeered by the ICA, there was a proposal to capture the Shelbourne Hotel, a high building overlooking the park. On the bank holiday it was full of guests, and it was probably for this reason that the idea was vetoed. Had the ICA taken over the hotel, they would have avoided the catastrophe on Tuesday morning when British Army machine gunners posted in the Shelbourne Hotel and United Services Club on the north side of the Green began to bombard the trenches, killing at least four insurgents.

BRITISH TROOPS behind impromptu barricades. Bizarrely, during the Rising, fire was temporarily halted to allow the nearby park's groundsman to feed the ducks.

Several civilians had been killed by the St Stephen's Green garrison so far, some for refusing to give up their vehicles to form a barricade and some in the crossfire.

Mallin led a retreat from the north side of St Stephen's Green, furthest from the Shelbourne's guns, to the Royal College of Surgeons, where the insurgents stayed for the rest of Easter week. Solidly made, the college was peppered with machine gun fire that did not penetrate the walls and the garrison was safe inside. However, there was barely any food and though a runner to Jacob's Biscuit Factory brought back welcome rations of chocolate cake, after several days the rebels were famished. Though about 12 other small rebel strongholds were established in and around the Green, by the end of the week the British had retaken many of them and had succeeded in isolating Mallin's garrison. Spirits were low when, on the orders of James Connolly, delivered from the GPO, the garrison surrendered on Sunday morning. Mallin was executed with the other leaders of the Rising. Constance Markievicz escaped with a death sentence commuted to life imprisonment because she was a woman.

A GRAND GESTURE
When she had to disarm as part of the surrender of the garrison, Constance Markievicz kissed her pistol before handing it over.

Tuesday 25 April: British Troops Deployed from the Curragh

A crucial element in how events over Easter week played out was the failure of the rebels to secure Amiens Street (now Connolly) railway station and Kingsbridge (now Heuston) railway station, which the British military used to bring reinforcements from the Curragh in Kildare and Belfast.

PHOTOGRAPH BY W.J. Westropp of the scene at O'Connell Bridge after the fighting, showing extensive damage.

Additionally, though some of the bridges in Dublin were held by rebels to limit the movements of their enemies, some had no rebel presence at all. This

allowed the British military to cordon off the insurgents in the north of the city from those in the south and isolate them in their positions.

Caught unprepared, the British forces had been at a serious disadvantage; as Easter Monday was a holiday, there had been only 400 men in nine different garrisons across the city available to fight out of a total of 2,400 troops in Ireland at the time. On Tuesday 25 April special troop trains brought over 1,600 troops from the Curragh to Kingsbridge railway station, followed by a further 1,000 under the command of Brigadier General William Lowe. General Lowe's arrival in Dublin was a vindication for Lord Wimbourne, Lord Lieutenant of Ireland. Wimbourne declared martial law, and handed over command of the British military forces to Lowe, because the current chief of military operations in Ireland, Major General Sir Lovick Friend, was in London for Easter. Before leaving London

TROOPS
stationed at City Hall.

to make his hasty return to Dublin, General Friend ordered 10,000 British soldiers from their camp at St Albans in England to Dublin to support the British forces there. The plan was that there would be no concerted action until reinforcements arrived, but after that the response would be swift and intense.

BRITISH SOLDIERS firing from an impromptu barricade of furniture and other assorted items.

By Tuesday evening the British troops at the Shelbourne Hotel had forced Mallin's rebels out of St Stephen's Green, so almost 4,000 British soldiers were now freed up for duty elsewhere in the city. By

that night the British had cordoned off the north side of the city and had gained control of two vital lines running across the city centre – one from Kingsbridge railway station to Dublin Castle in the west and the other from Trinity College to the Custom House in the east. City Hall had also been captured, meaning Dublin Castle was now safe.

BRITISH SOLDIERS
stationed in Dublin.

TRINITY COLLEGE

It is unclear why the rebels never attempted to take Trinity College, the largely unionist college in the centre of Dublin city and a mere five minutes from the GPO. However, Trinity did play its part in the 1916 Rising. The college's own Dublin University Officer Training Corps, along with some of its students, defended the college until British troops, the South Staffordshires, arrived on Wednesday evening and took it as their base.

Tuesday 25 April: The World's First Radio Broadcast

Meanwhile, the Provisional Government stationed in the GPO was keen to tell the world of the declaration of an Irish Republic.

FERGUS O'KELLY
repairing a ship's transmitter.

As the British had cut the telephone and telegraph lines at the start of the Rising, Joseph Plunkett sent out a squadron of hand-picked Irish Volunteers from the GPO to occupy a wireless training school that had been shut down at the outbreak of World War I.

The equipment had been dismantled but the squad of men sent included Fergus O'Kelly, who had served in the Army Signal Corps. He managed to repair a ship's transmitter used by the school for training. Another squad member, David Bourke, was experienced in broadcasting in Morse code, and at 5:30 p.m. on Tuesday 25 April he started sending the following message to anyone who could receive it: 'Irish Republic declared in Dublin today, Irish troops have captured the city and are in full possession. Enemy cannot move in city.

JOSEPH PLUNKETT
operating the wireless
radio from the GPO
training centre.

HMS *ADVENTURE*
The 12th in a line of ships of the same name in the British Royal Navy.

The whole country rising.' This was in fact the world's first radio broadcast; broadcasts had previously only been sent from one point to another, not out on all channels to whomever might be listening. The messages the rebels sent were received in parts of Europe and by ships, some of which brought the news to America, and one of which, the British warship HMS *Adventure* was anchored at Dún Laoghaire. Unfortunately, the rebels never knew that anyone had received their signals – though the transmitter was now working, the receiver remained out of order until the building was burnt out on Easter Wednesday. A message sent earlier that day read rather optimistically, given the bemused and hostile reception of the locals to the Rising: 'British troops have been repulsed with great slaughter in the attempt to take the Irish position. The people are wildly enthusiastic for the new government.'

THE 'SEPARATION WOMEN'

The so-called 'separation women' were family members – generally the wives – of Irishmen who were fighting in the British army in World War I. They strongly and sometimes violently rejected the legitimacy of the rebels' actions. To these women, whose families were often poor and completely reliant on income from the British army, and whose loved ones were fighting in extremely dangerous conditions in France, the Rising was a galling spectacle. At the GPO, St Stephen's Green, Jacob's Biscuit Factory and many more locations, separation women and other onlookers hurled abuse at the Irish Volunteers and ICA. The photo below shows a scene of devastation at Elvery's, Hotel Metropole and Post Office, Sackville Street, 18 May, taken by W.J. Westropp.

Wednesday 26 April:
The Rising in Wexford

The Rising in Enniscorthy, unlike that in Dublin, proceeded with a remarkable lack of bloodshed.

A SCENE IN WEXFORD, where there was little bloodshed.

After the countermand sent by Eoin MacNeill, the Wexford Volunteers received the message 'we start at noon today, obey your orders'. As it was not clear what the orders were, Captain Paul Galligan travelled to Dublin and met with James Connolly at the GPO to confirm. Connolly ordered them to capture the railway line from Rosslare to prevent British reinforcements reaching Dublin. The Enniscorthy contingent, along with other Volunteer brigades from surrounding small towns, proceeded to take over Enniscorthy. They established their headquarters in the

Athenaeum theatre, where Pádraig Pearse had made a stirring speech the previous month. The railway line and roads were blocked, and the local RIC barracks was surrounded; Galligan also took the small town of Ferns and the northern part of the county.

PAUL GALLIGAN
After meeting with Connolly at the GPO, Captain Galligan cycled back to Enniscorthy by a circuitous 200-kilometre route to evade capture.

Unlike the Dublin Rising, the majority of the population supported the Rising – there was a high rate of trade union activism and national feeling and one of the local priests, Father Patrick Murphy, was an open supporter of the nationalists.

By Saturday the insurgents numbered almost 1,000 and British forces were mobilising to engage them. When the District Inspector came with Pearse's surrender order on Sunday morning, the officers did not believe it to be genuine. With the permission of the British military, they travelled to Dublin to meet with Pearse in Arbour Hill Prison to have the news confirmed. On Monday morning they surrendered unconditionally.

Wednesday 26 April: The Arrival of the Gun Boat *Helga*

On Wednesday more heavy guns arrived from a different quarter: the patrol vessel *Helga* sailed up the Liffey from the port at Kingstown to shell Liberty Hall.

LIMITED FIRE
The *Helga* fired only 40 rounds during the Rising and had to stop firing as her shells were endangering the Viceregal Lodge (now Áras an Uachtaráin, the residence of the President of Ireland) in Phoenix Park.

Though the *Helga* was equipped with a 12-pounder coastal defence gun, she was originally designed as a fishery research ship and was co-opted by the British Admiralty at the start of World War I.

At around 8:00 a.m. on Wednesday the *Helga* tied up on the south quays opposite the Custom House and began shelling the now completely empty Liberty Hall in the mistaken belief that there were still rebels

inside. The constant ear-shattering sound of the shells, coupled with those fired from the heavy 18-pounder guns at Trinity College, led the garrison at the GPO to believe they were under attack. However, they soon realised that Liberty Hall was burning, though the difficult angle of fire for the *Helga* meant that this was more attributable to direct hits by some of the Trinity College guns.

LIBERTY HALL
The rebels' headquarters.

In 1923 the *Helga* was handed over to the Irish Free State as one of the first ships of the Irish Navy and renamed the *Muirchú* (Sea Hound). However, later that year she was returned to her original purpose of fishery and marine research and after this became used for coast-guard duties. While she was being taken to Dublin to be scrapped in 1947, she sank off the Saltee Islands.

Wednesday 26 April: British Reinforcements Land at Kingstown

On Easter Monday Commandant Éamon de Valera set out to capture Boland's Mill, a flour mill just off Grand Canal Dock.

The Boland's Mill garrison had a large area to secure and few men, so Lieutenant Michael Malone, a 28-year-old carpenter, took 14 men and held the area around Mount Street Bridge, including No. 25 Haddington Road and Clanwilliam House, a large three-storey Georgian building that had excellent views of Mount Street Bridge. It was vital that the bridge be held as this was the route that the British reinforcements landing at Kingstown Port (now Dún Laoghaire) would use to move into Dublin.

This was because, although Amiens Street railway station and Kingsbridge railway station had fallen to the British, Captain McMahon's B Company of Volunteers managed to hold Westland Row railway station. British troops landing at Kingstown would therefore have to march into Dublin, passing the Mount Street force.

On Wednesday, word of thousands of these troops heading their way came to Malone. The British force was broadly made up of a regiment called the Sherwood Foresters, a force of raw recruits who had been in training for less than three months. Young and inexperienced, many did not know how to use their rifles, and upon landing at Kingstown, they were bemused to discover they were in Ireland rather than France. They were also taken aback when, upon marching into the city, local residents angry at the destruction wrought by the Rising, cheered and clapped them and appeared to be

LAST MEETING

As the Sherwood Foresters marched towards the city, Captain Frederick Dietrichsen, who had sent his wife and two children to Dublin to protect them from German air raids saw his family in the crowd. He stopped to hug them at the side of the road and then marched on with the rest of the men to Mount Street, where he was one of the first killed.

delighted to see them. Two of the battalions took a circuitous route around the city to enter from the west, making their way to Kilmainham Hospital and then on to Dublin Castle. The other two battalions received orders to march straight into Dublin, which brought them face to face with Malone's force.

As they marched over Mount Street Bridge, the first wave of Sherwood Foresters walked into a death trap, and were mown down in minutes. Unbelievably,

DRAMATIC SCENE
at Mount Street where many young British soliders were killed, from the RTÉ drama *Insurrection*, broadcast in 1966.

the green recruits were ordered to repeat the exercise. Wave after wave of soldiers armed with bayonets and rifles attempted to storm the bridge and were obliterated by rebel fire. Alarmed at such heavy losses, their commander, Brigadier Maconchy, requested that the troops find an alternative route (the forces could have passed the rebels easily if they moved along just one street), but General Lowe insisted that the bridge be taken 'at all costs'. Every 20 minutes successive waves of young, barely trained men started across the bridge only to be shot to pieces, and after nine hours 240 of them lay dead.

Eventually, through sheer force of numbers and the donation of a Lewis machine gun and hand grenades from the Dublin Military Garrison, the British troops succeeded in taking the bridge.

By 3:00 p.m. on Wednesday afternoon only nine rebels were still alive: two in No. 25 and seven in Clanwilliam House. No. 25 was overrun by military and Malone was shot dead, and Clanwilliam House took the brunt of the rest of the attack. At 8:00 p.m. that evening the Royal Naval Reserve drove a lorry containing a one-pounder gun up the street and set the building ablaze with incendiary shells. The four surviving rebels fled, two of them managing to evade capture and escape entirely by taking shelter in the grounds of a nearby convent until morning.

Wednesday 26 April: North King Street Area and Ned Daly

Commandant Edward John 'Ned' Daly had occupied the Four Courts and the surrounding areas on Easter Monday, 24 April, with a force of about 150 men.

As in outposts elsewhere across the city, MacNeill's countermand had resulted in much reduced numbers turning out, but what Daly's forces lacked in numbers they made up for in valour. In this they took after their commandant; Ned Daly was only 25 at the time of the Rising and the youngest in the nationalist forces to hold that rank, but despite a family connection to Tom Clarke (Clarke's wife was Daly's older sister), he earned his rank through talent and drive.

The importance of the Four Courts for the rebels was primarily that it was the perfect location to prevent British reinforcements from the Royal Barracks to the west of the city and Kingsbridge railway station

EDWARD DALY,
the youngest commandant of the 1916 Rising.

moving in eastwards towards the GPO. Daly's was a large area to hold with so few men, stretching from Cabra and the North Circular Road in the north to the Mendicity Institution in the south, but his garrison was well-prepared. The bulk of the men were from some of the poorest areas of the north side and had been trained in hand-to-hand combat. The surrounding area had been thoroughly reconnoitred by Daly so the

FOUR COURTS
The British soldiers held as prisoners were impressed with their treatment at the Four Courts, finding Ned Daly's men both courteous and honourable.

garrison were familiar with the key targets, the best positions and sources of provisions for the days ahead.

To buy Daly's garrison some time, another 25-year-old, Seán Heuston, led a small party to capture the Mendicity Institution, a stately building that housed a free meal distribution service for the poor.

On Easter Monday Daly's forces stormed the Four Courts, which was all but empty on the bank holiday. Daly's first engagement was a victorious clash with a party of British cavalry, who were escorting lorries loaded with ammunition. In the Mendicity Institution, after scattering forces from the Royal Barracks, the rebels found themselves in a siege situation. On Tuesday, amazed that the Mendicity Institution was still being held, James Connolly sent 12 men to reinforce their garrison, taking it to 26 in total, but the British were closing in and on Wednesday Heuston was forced to surrender to save the lives of his men.

Also on Wednesday Daly captured two enemy positions in the area, the Bridewell Barracks and the Linenhall Barracks. In the Bridewell, 25 policemen were found lying low in the cells. They were marched back to the Four Courts as prisoners. In the Linenhall, the rebels found 32 unarmed army clerks.

By Thursday the South Staffordshires and Sherwood

Foresters were closing in and fierce fighting ensued, particularly in the North King Street area. While Daly was very conscientious in attempting to protect civilians, securing Monks's bakery and arranging for bread to be distributed, a number of civilians were murdered by soldiers of the South Staffordshire regiment under Colonel Henry Taylor. Maddened by heavy casualties, with nothing to show for it, they broke into houses on North King Street and shot or bayoneted 15 civilian men in a vicious act of revenge. The fighting continued until Saturday evening when Pearse's surrender was confirmed.

PHOTOGRAPH of the devastation in North King street taken by T.W. Murphy.

Wednesday 26 April: Sackville Street Shelled

James Connolly's plan had been to trap the British forces in the city as the Irish Volunteers from the rest of the country moved in. By Wednesday, this was no longer an option, so Connolly fell to his back-up plan.

JAMES CONNOLLY'S men occupied buildings and fought running battles.

Believing that the British, as committed capitalists, would never sanction the damage of private property such as would occur if they employed artillery, Connolly anticipated hand-to-hand fighting in the streets, and so his tactic was to occupy various buildings around O'Connell Street, in many cases boring holes through their party walls so their forces could pass up and down unmolested.

The garrison in the GPO had now almost doubled its numbers to approximately 300, made up of ICA and Volunteer latecomers collected from Liberty Hall by a Volunteer transferring arms and munitions from there to the GPO and augmented by ordinary citizens and a handful of other groups who wished to join the Rising.

On Tuesday afternoon, to bolster the spirits of the garrison, Pearse read a manifesto on Sackville Street declaring that republican forces were holding their own against the British military and – untruthfully – that the rest of the country was rising in support.

By noon on Tuesday the building opposite the GPO housing Clery's department store and the Imperial Hotel was under fire. The Imperial Hotel was owned by William Martin Murphy, the anti-trade unionist who had locked out the workers during the Dublin Lockout in 1913. He was Connolly's nemesis, so Connolly took great care to have the Starry Plough, the flag of the ICA, run up its flagpole. British snipers reacted by directing fire at the hotel.

BRITISH SOLDIERS firing upon rebel positions from an impromptu barricade.

GUNNERS
British troops used artillery against the rebels.

On Wednesday the *Helga* destroyed Liberty Hall, and soon British gunners on the roofs of Trinity College were peppering O'Connell Street with machine gun fire, pinning the rebels in their positions.

Shells from Trinity College's heavy guns forced the rebels occupying Kelly's gun shop at the west corner of Sackville Street facing onto the Liffey to fall back to the GPO.

The garrison holding the Metropole Hotel, the building to the right of the GPO, was increased, and the rebels managed also to break through into Eason's stationers, giving them further control of the area. On Wednesday, although word of the Mount

Street victory came through, it was clear to the GPO garrison, from leaders to rank-and-file, that as the rest of the country had not risen and the British were pouring reinforcements into the city, they would not be victorious. Yet morale remained high – the forces in the GPO expected the end to come, and from this point on, they considered themselves to be making the ultimate sacrifice for Ireland.

SCENE OF DESTRUCTON at the Hotel Metropole, Dublin, May 1916.

Thursday 27 April: Jacob's Biscuit Factory

The factory seemed an incongruous base for the insurgents, but in fact it was perfect – a huge building with towers giving excellent views over the city, located in a nest of lanes, halfway between two British barracks and Dublin Castle.

Commanded by Thomas MacDonagh, a poet, dramatist and University College Dublin lecturer, MacDonagh was somewhat erratic as a commander. The second-in-command at Jacob's was John MacBride, estranged husband of Maud Gonne and the man immortalised by the words of W.B. Yeats in his poem 'Easter 1916' as 'this man I had dreamed a drunken inglorious lout'. When his successful career in the British military ended 15 years earlier, MacBride had taken to drink, and, although he was a member of the IRB, he had not been thought sufficiently trustworthy to have the plans for the Rising shared with him. Nevertheless, he proved to be in possession of a cool head and steady pair of hands, with which he steered MacDonagh in the right direction throughout the week.

JACOB'S BISCUIT FACTORY
was a redoubt of the rebels during the fighting.

The area around Jacob's was one of the most pro-British in the city – crowds of separation women booed and kicked at the Volunteers as they made their way to the factory, and after the gates of the factory had been closed behind them, it was necessary to fire blanks to disperse them. There was no real fighting at Jacob's except

in the first hour of the occupation, when approximately 30 British soldiers were shot at as they moved down Camden Street. As the factory was not of strategic importance to the British, General Lowe decided to concentrate on the GPO and the Four Courts. However, the endless waiting, sniper fire, and sleeplessness took their toll on the garrison. Additionally, though some Cumann na mBan women did their best to supplement the diet with what meat and vegetables could be scavenged from around the area, the main ration was cake – of which the Volunteers were soon heartily sick.

MacDonagh regularly cherry-picked the news he relayed to his garrison, painting a positive picture of success, less out of malice than wishful thinking. As the week went on and it became obvious that the insurgents were losing, the rumour mill created more fantastic claims every day.

It was Sunday before word of the surrender made its way to Jacob's, brought by Nurse Elizabeth O'Farrell. Initially MacDonagh refused to surrender, and it required a persuasive talk at a meeting arranged by General Lowe before he could be convinced that all was lost, and surrender was the only option.

DRAWING OF JACOB'S BISCUIT FACTORY
from a 1920s handbook of Dublin published by the Corporation of Dublin.

JACOB'S BISCUIT FACTORY
depicted in a pictorial magazine of the time.

Thursday 27 April: Boland's Mill Shootout

The area around Boland's Bakery and Flour Mill, which overlooks Grand Canal Dock, was targeted by the rebels as it was just south of the GPO and had control of the railway line and main road from Kingstown Port, where the British were bound to import their reinforcements.

Boland's Mill was taken as the headquarters of the garrison, with outposts as satellites. Éamon de Valera was the Commandant of the 3rd Battalion earmarked to take the area, which comprised Westland Row railway station, Boland's Mill, the nearby Boland's Bakery, an adjacent poor law dispensary, a building yard by Grand Canal Dock, and multiple locations around Mount Street Bridge. A clever, somewhat ascetic man born in New York but raised by his Irish grandmother in County Limerick, de Valera was a teacher by profession. He had been recruited from the Irish Volunteers into the IRB by Thomas MacDonagh.

De Valera had hoped for at least 500 men, but the turnout on Easter Monday was dismal after MacNeill's countermand of the day before, with only approximately 170 soldiers reporting for duty – not sufficient to cover such a wide area. Worse than that, the company had no quartermaster and only 50 rifles between them, with bullets of a different make which did not quite fit, causing them to have to constantly reload. The rest made do with shotguns or pistols.

De Valera's cleverness was best demonstrated by his inspired idea for directing fire on Boland's Mill from the *Helga*, using a British naval gun that had been taken ashore from the ship and set up nearby. Short of men, de Valera sent those in an abandoned distillery

SURRENDER

Beggars Bush Barracks was successfully kept pinned down until orders to surrender came on Saturday and de Valera's fears that civilians would be harmed were realised. The photo below shows the view towards the barracks taken in the 1930s.

nearby back to base. To avoid the high building being taken by the British, he ordered Captain Michael Cullen to climb the tower and, with the tricolour, pretend to send semaphore messages. The British assumed this was a rebel headquarters and concentrated most of their fire on this building.

There was no significant fighting at Boland's Mill, apart from the Mount Street battle, until Thursday, yet the sniper fire had been continuous and the net was closing in; at this point, despite urgings from de Valera to stay alert, the garrison was exhausted and becoming demoralised when it became clear that the Rising would not be successful. By Thursday, de Valera had not slept in days and was behaving erratically – the men were deeply affected by an incident on Thursday night when one man, ordered to be quiet after constantly talking while others tried to sleep, shot and killed his superior officer before himself being killed. On Friday the British continued to close in. Despite plentiful food the rebels went hungry as they were too pinned down by sniper fire to distribute it. Saturday was uneventful, and on Sunday Nurse O'Farrell arrived carrying an urgent message from Pearse that the Rising was over. Perhaps indicative of his distrust of women, initially de Valera did not believe her and refused to obey the surrender until MacDonagh, his commandant, countersigned the document.

CUMANN NA MBAN ARE EXCLUDED

De Valera felt that women had no place on a battlefield – even female soldiers. Despite the lack of resource at the Boland's Mill area, de Valera deliberately did not send a courier to collect a force of Cumann na mBan women at their Merrion Square meeting point, leaving some to go home and some to join MacDonagh's forces in Jacob's Biscuit Factory. The photo below shows Cumann na mBan women protesting in 1921 for the release of prisoners.

24–29 April: The Rising in Galway

The issuing of the order to mobilise, then the countermand, and then word from Pearse on Monday to mobilise had created particular confusion amongst the ranks of the Galway Volunteers.

LIAM MELLOWS
disguised himself as a priest to return to Ireland to lead attacks on RIC stations.

Pearse had commanded them to carry out their orders, but the command to meet arms coming up from Tralee and begin a rising west of the Shannon no longer made sense after the failure of the *Aud* to deliver its cargo. The RIC in Galway city were on alert, and so the main rebel activity in Galway occurred rurally. Liam Mellows, the son of a British army soldier, was just 24 at the time of the 1916 Rising, but was a founding member of the Irish Volunteers and had been member of the IRB for years. Just before the Rising he was in England under an exclusion order, but he arrived back in Ireland on Easter Monday disguised as a priest to find a strong but poorly armed turnout in Galway of up to 1,000 men.

Mellows led several abortive attacks on RIC stations, including those at Oranmore and Clarinbridge, and then proceeded to Athenry where he used the agricultural college near the town centre as the base of rebel operations. On Wednesday, two companies of Galway Volunteers routed a military detachment travelling from Galway to Athenry, but their success was short-lived – badly armed and poorly supplied with provisions, and under pressure from more and more British troops, the officers held conferences to consider disbanding on Thursday and again on Friday. In the meantime the British cruisers *Laburnum* and *Gloucester* were sent to Galway harbour, where the *Laburnum* shelled the city. Early on Saturday a local priest brought news that the Rising in Dublin was on the verge of collapse, and the Galway Volunteers finally agreed to disperse. Mellows escaped to the United States while the rank and file dispersed to their homes. During the War of Independence, Mellows became the Irish Republican Army Director of Supplies, purchasing arms for the forces, and was elected to the First Dáil in 1918 as a Sinn Féin TD.

HMS *LABURNUM*
painted in WWI dazzle camouflage colours.

ÉAMONN CEANNT
joined the Gaelic League in 1899, where he met others, such as Pádraig Pearse, who were to become prominent in the 1916 Rising.

Thursday 28 April: Cathal Brugha Wounded at the South Dublin Union

The taking of the huge complex of the South Dublin Union was led by Éamonn Ceannt, a taciturn, sober and devoutly Catholic member of the IRB Military Council.

The South Dublin Union was located in the west of the city close to Kingsbridge railway station, and the Wellington, Islandbridge and Richmond Barracks, and the Royal Hospital; this was not in fact in use as a hospital, but was the headquarters of the British military. It was the largest poorhouse in Ireland, a sprawling complex containing three hospitals, accommodation for the large staff of doctors and nurses, and administrative buildings, located in 50 acres of green space. It housed more than 3,000 poor or elderly citizens – Ceannt tried to keep them out of harm's way during the fighting, though inevitably there were casualties.

After entering the South Dublin Union, Ceannt initially made his headquarters in an area vulnerable to the sniper fire that was soon hitting the building, but quickly moved to the night nurses' home, which was close to the James's Street entrance. He kept half his 120-strong force with him and split the rest into three groups of 20, each led by an officer, and assigned them various outposts around the complex. Ceannt's command was characterised by sharp strategy and extreme bravery. His second-in-command was Cathal Brugha, a long-time nationalist as austere and fearless as Ceannt himself. On Monday a side gate was breached by British soldiers, and from that point on the fighting was hand-to-hand and often room-to-room, with danger around every corner.

MEDICAL AID
Several among the staff and patients of the South Dublin Union aided the rebels – Nurse Margaretta Keogh volunteered to help by tending the wounded, and was shot by British troops.

Heavy sniper fire was experienced on Tuesday, while inside the nurses' home a barricade reinforced with rubble was constructed. Wednesday was eerily quiet – the calm before the storm. On Thursday the British launched a major offensive, bombarding the nurses' home first with sniper fire, then with rifle fire, machine gun fire and grenades, reinforced by the two battalions of the Sherwood Foresters, who had reached Dublin from the west, avoiding the carnage at Mount Street.

A grenade blast critically wounded Brugha, who ordered his men to retreat and leave him. They obeyed, only for Ceannt to hear him cursing the British soldiers. Bloody but unbowed, Brugha was sitting with his revolver cocked ready to shoot when they returned. That evening the British called off their attack, and Brugha's multiple wounds were tended. He had 25 separate wounds and was not expected to last the night, but he did survive, though he was left with a permanent limp.

From Friday on, there were no more large-scale attacks, though sniper fire continued; General Lowe had prioritised crushing the rebellion at the GPO and the Four Courts. It was Sunday before the order to surrender came to Ceannt; the garrison was tempted to hold out and continue fighting, but after some discussion they decided to surrender.

IRISH ACTOR
Joe Lynch as Cathal Brugha (left) and an unidentified actor, in a scene from the RTÉ drama series *Insurrection* during studio filming in early 1966.

THOMAS ASHE
was principal of
Corduff National
School, Lusk,
County Dublin. He
commanded the
Fingal battalion
of the Irish
Volunteeers.

Friday 28 April:
The Rising in Ashbourne

During the Rising, the North County Dublin Volunteers (5th Battalion) under Kerry-born teacher Commandant Thomas Ashe was the most active of the non city-centre based Volunteer branches.

Operating rurally, their mission was to damage railway lines and capture police barracks in order to source arms, scupper British military plans and support the rest of the Irish Volunteers in Dublin city.

After a few days of disorganisation owing to Ashe's lack of military experience and the men's demoralisation at the small size of their approximately 50-strong company, the garrison was transformed by the arrival on Tuesday of Richard Mulcahy, a lieutenant from the 3rd Battalion. Mulcahy made the inspired suggestion to split into four groups of 11 men, each with an officer – a 'flying column' formation that became common in the guerilla warfare of the War of Independence.

Starting in the village of Swords, from Wednesday onwards the Volunteers captured several police stations, seizing weapons and smashing what they could, and on Friday morning the remaining 40 split into three groups to destroy the railway line near Batterstown, disrupting the movement of British troops into the city.

A POEM
by Thomas Ashe, who went to prison in Lewes, England.

SWORDS VILLAGE, DUBLIN,
where four civilians were killed in the battle, as well as two Volunteers, John Crennigan and Thomas Rafferty.

DAVID LLOYD GEORGE
Prime Minister of the United Kingdom at the time of the 1916 Rising.

As they moved in on the town, scouts encountered three fully armed RIC constables on bicycles, and captured them. They were sent back to the barracks to demand a full surrender to the rebels, but an attempted attack had been expected, and the usual small force had been augmented by more troops. After a fierce gun battle the police inside the barracks surrendered. However, just as this happened, 15 cars holding 55 RIC reinforcements arrived from Slane and the barracks rescinded their surrender. Taken by surprise to have run straight into the rebel forces, the RIC were at a disadvantage, and Mulcahy pressed his advantage home and attacked. After some hours of fighting in which approximately 15 police officers were killed, one of whom was District Inspector Harry Smith, the constables surrendered and were taken prisoner.

The victory was short-lived. The next day, Saturday, Ashe received confirmation of Pearse's surrender at the GPO. After the Rising Ashe was court-martialled and sentenced to death, but the sentence was commuted to penal servitude for life. He and fellow prisoners

Éamon de Valera and Thomas Hunter led a hunger strike in May 1917 in protest at the mistreatment of the prisoners who had fought in the Rising. Public feeling caused Prime Minister Lloyd George to declare a general amnesty and the remaining prisoners were released on 18 June 1917.

In August 1917, Ashe was rearrested, convicted of sedition and sentenced to two years' hard labour. Denied prisoner-of-war status, Ashe again went on hunger strike. He died of pneumonia after having been deprived of his bedding and his boots by the prison authorities and then force-fed in his weakened state.

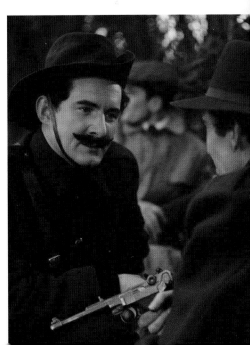

JOHN O'FLYNN
as Thomas Ashe during the filming of the Battle of Ashbourne scene from the RTÉ drama series *Insurrection*.

Friday 28 April: The GPO Abandoned

Thursday dawned bright and clear to an ever-tightening cordon around the GPO.

The British held many of the adjacent locations, including Liberty Hall, Amiens Street and from Parnell Place to Findlater's Place, as well as Trinity College and College Street. From dawn, a firefight had been raging between the teams of snipers on the roof of the GPO and the British machine gunners and snipers. Shells bombarded the Metropole Hotel, which had to be abandoned, and neighbouring buildings, but the GPO had not yet suffered a direct hit. Pádraig Pearse made a rousing speech to the GPO garrison, reinforcing what they had achieved – successfully holding out as a republic for three days – but also falsely claiming that there was still hope in the form of Volunteer reinforcements on their way from Dundalk.

THE GPO EXODUS
At 8:00 p.m. the Volunteers finally left the GPO, slipping out in groups from the Henry Street exit into the chaos of the streets, making for Ned Daly's garrison at the Four Courts.

On Thursday James Connolly was hit in the leg by a sniper bullet on his way back from establishing outposts at Liffey Street, a serious wound that shattered his shinbone. Dosed with morphine, he was incapacitated for the rest of the day and The O'Rahilly took over practical command of the soldiers, with Tom Clarke and Seán MacDermott in support. Pearse, who had not slept all week, was clearly suffering from exhaustion.

That afternoon the British began a bombardment with howitzers, heavy artillery guns that fired shrapnel shells at the GPO. Later that evening incendiary shells followed, setting most of the buildings on the eastern side of Sackville Street ablaze. It was now impossible for the rebels to send or receive any dispatches from other locations – they were well and truly on their own.

On Friday morning the full extent of the damage to the GPO was obvious, and as the afternoon wore on the British pressed home their advantage, sending incendiary shells into the GPO until the garrison, constantly fighting the fires breaking out everywhere, had to evacuate. Women and the wounded were evacuated first, and then The O'Rahilly took a band of 25 men to secure the Williams & Woods jam factory in Great Britain Street (now Parnell Street). He was cut down by fire when he was trying to rejoin his men, from whom he had become separated.

Friday 28 April: Clery's Department Store and the Imperial Hotel on Sackville Street Collapse

CLERY'S

In 1922 the building was rebuilt to a design by the world-famous architect, Robert Atkinson. Atkinson also designed London's Selfridges, with which it has many similarities.

James Connolly could not have been more wrong in his belief that the capitalist British would baulk at destroying private property.

Clery's Department Store and the Imperial Hotel were owned by William Martin Murphy, Connolly's long-time enemy and the chief antagonist of the 1913 Dublin Lockout.

The incendiary shells that had battered Sackville Street on Thursday evening also claimed Clery's and the Imperial. Oscar Traynor, the commander of the garrison stationed at the Metropole, a hotel beside the GPO, recalled that James

Connolly had ordered a barricade to be
built on Lower Abbey Street. As he and
his garrison looked on, it caught fire after
an incendiary hit it. The flames spread
to a neighbouring building and then,
disastrously, on to Hoyte's. Hoyte's was
a chemist's shop with an oil and glass
warehouse. It was a perfect tinderbox
that went up in a spectacular flash,
spitting tongues of multicoloured flame.

**THE IMPERIAL
HOTEL**
Sackville
Street, 18 May
1916, showing
the façade,
photographed by
W.J. Westropp.

   The thick, acrid smoke was choking,
but as Clery's and the Imperial Hotel caught fire,
the heat was unbearable. The plate glass of the iconic
department store, designed in the mid-19th century,
to be a match for any of the grand stores on the
Continent, melted from the intensity of the heat, and
water poured on the barricades at the GPO turned to
steam despite its distance from the other buildings.

   Overnight the buildings collapsed entirely, and the
next morning all that was left of the grand old 1853
building was its façade.

Friday 28 April:
General Maxwell and the Imposition of Martial Law

GENERAL JOHN MAXWELL (left of centre) reviewing British reserve soldiers in Trinity College Dublin after the 1916 Rising. The reserve corps' motto was 'Georgius Rex'. Dubliners knew them as the Gorgeous Wrecks.

On the first day of the 1916 Rising, Lord Wimbourne, Lord Lieutenant of Ireland, declared martial law. In the absence of Major General Lovick Friend, chief of military operations in Ireland, who was in London for Easter, the Lord Lieutenant transferred power to Brigadier General William Lowe.

In the view of the British military, General Friend had to be replaced, so Prime Minister Herbert Asquith selected General John Maxwell as overall commander, a seemingly solid choice, for the job of putting down the Rising. Though he had served at British army headquarters in the Royal Hospital, Kilmainham for two years, General Maxwell had no military experience in Ireland, but he had served with honour in Egypt, the Sudan and South Africa.

General Maxwell arrived in the small hours of the morning of Friday 28 April to a city in flames. He immediately set about containing any further outposts with the now almost 20,000 strong British military forces at his command. Friday's intensive shelling of the GPO was part of General Maxwell's plan to focus on the rebels' headquarters and force them from their positions.

General Maxwell would accept only unconditional surrender and had no sympathy for the rebels' cause – rather than patriots or soldiers, he regarded them as lawbreakers, saying: 'Most rigorous measures will be taken by me to stop the loss of life and damage to property which certain misguided persons are causing by their armed resistance to the law.'

Friday 28 April:
Last Stand on Moore Street

MICHAEL O'RAHILLY
Photographed in 1916, known as The O'Rahilly.

As the GPO garrison left the burning building, Pádraig Pearse ducked back inside to check that no-one had been left behind.

He intended to be the last man out, but though the building seemed clear, there were actually two men still left in the basement, who were surprised to find the building abandoned when they came back upstairs. Just before 8:00 p.m. the garrison was waiting tensely for the signal to move, and on the stroke of eight poured from the exit into Henry Street to be met by a hail of bullets coming from all directions. The Volunteer force of nearly 300 made a panicked break for Moore Street with a view to joining Ned Daly's forces at the Four Courts, but in the confusion, and with a feverish but uncomplaining James Connolly being conveyed on a stretcher, nobody seemed to be in command. The company ran straight into the talented 20-year-old Volunteer scout Seán McLoughlin, who, while mystified to see what looked to be the whole company running towards him, swiftly took charge, directing them to Henry Place, a narrow laneway where there was some shelter. McLoughlin raced off after The O'Rahilly to warn him that Great Britain Street was entirely under British control and a hopeless cause, but the battered remnants of his task force informed him that The O'Rahilly had been shot down with 21 of his men.

With Connolly's permission, McLoughlin took charge, promising, 'I can get you out of here, but there will be only one man giving the orders and I will give them.' A van was pushed across the mouth of Moore Lane to screen the Volunteers from British fire as they dashed from the lane into Moore Street. One by one they made the run against a spurt of gunfire, and eventually the garrison broke into Moore Street houses to take shelter against the constant fire. Connolly and some members of the Provisional Government, as well as Nurse Elizabeth O'Farrell, took shelter in Cogan's corner shop (No. 12). O'Farrell was one of only three members of Cumann na mBan allowed by Pearse to stay with the main garrison as it evacuated, the others being Winifred Carney and Julia Grenan.

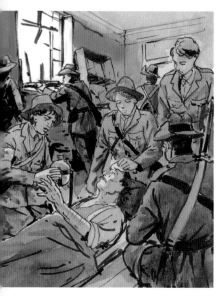

O'Farrell approached Connolly, lying on a stretcher, and asked him how he felt. He answered, 'Bad'. For a man such as Connolly, this admission could not be taken lightly. In a meeting with the Provisional Government that night, McLoughlin was made Commandant-General on the advice of Connolly and charged with creating an escape plan.

McLoughlin ordered the men to start burrowing through the walls of the tenements, working in relays, and by daybreak the burrowing party had reached Sackville Lane (now O'Rahilly Parade). McLoughlin then suggested an attack on the nearby British barricades by a 'death or glory' squad of 30 that would draw the British fire while the others escaped.

JAMES CONNOLLY
survived long enough to be executed by the British six days later, suffering from gangrene.

THE BURNT-OUT
remains of The O'Rahilly's De Dion Bouton, used as part of a makeshift barricade in Prince's Street, Dublin.

Saturday 29 April: The Volunteer Leaders Surrender

As Seán McLoughlin was recruiting for his 'death or glory' squad, Pearse was having grave doubts; on Friday he had watched British soldiers gun down a group of women and had seen a family who feared their house was catching fire mown down in the street, their white flag notwithstanding.

NURSE ELIZABETH O'FARRELL
walking up Moore Street with a white handkerchief to signal surrender.

Those members of the Provisional Government present – Pearse, Connolly, Clarke, MacDermott and Plunkett – held their last council of war in Hanlon's fish shop at 16 Moore Street on Saturday morning. After a long meeting only the fierce old Fenian Tom Clarke held out for continuing the fight; outvoted, he wept at the final decision to surrender.

Upon being told the news and ordered to stand down his squad, McLoughlin did not take things well, nor did MacDermott's men when he told them. However, the signatories to the Proclamation suspected that they would face a firing squad, while the junior officers and rank and file would be released, and they emphasised to the men that the nationalist movement needed them to live to fight another day. Connolly told McLoughlin: 'You will have plenty to do in the future, if you keep quiet … we have done our best.' Volunteer Jim Ryan reported that after speaking to MacDermott, Clarke and Plunkett he suspected that 'these men agreed amongst themselves before Pearse went to the Castle that they should offer their own lives in an attempt to save those of their followers.'

At 12:45 p.m. Nurse Elizabeth O'Farrell stepped out of the doorway of No. 15 carrying a white handkerchief on a stick and walked up Moore Street to the British barricade. She repeated a message from Pearse that he wished to discuss terms of surrender and was taken to General Lowe, who had made a temporary base at Clarke's tobacconist stand. In line with General Maxwell's strict policy of unconditional surrender, General Lowe wrote a note to Pearse asking for his decision in half an hour, and brought Nurse O'Farrell

SHEELAGH CULLEN as Elizabeth O'Farrell and Eoin Ó Súilleabháin as Pádraig Pearse, approach a British Army barricade in a scene from the RTÉ drama *Insurrection*, during location filming on Little Mary Street, Dublin, in early 1966.

PÁDRAIG PEARSE surrendering to General Lowe, with Nurse Elizabeth O'Farrell at his side.

back to Moore Street in his own car. Eventually, after failing to secure any other terms, Pearse surrendered unconditionally.

Six days after the inception of the Provisional Government, Pearse walked up Moore Street with O'Farrell by his side and gave his sword, pistol and signature of surrender to General Lowe. O'Farrell accepted the charge of bringing the surrender command to the rest of the outposts, and Pearse was taken to meet General Maxwell where he was required to sign a formal surrender notice. The notice read: '*In order to prevent further slaughter of the civil population and in the hope of saving the lives of our followers, the members of the Provisional Government present at headquarters have decided on an unconditional surrender, and commandants or officers commanding districts will order their commands to lay down arms. P. H. Pearse, Dublin 30th April 1916.*'

The rest of the garrison in Moore Street marched

to Sackville Street, where they laid down their weapons before being brought to the grounds of the Rotunda Hospital. They stayed there overnight, outside in the bitter cold in very cramped conditions, which were made yet more cramped when Ned Daly's Four Courts garrison joined them. In the morning they were given an armed military escort to Richmond Barracks. With their city reduced to rubble and their loved ones fighting in the trenches betrayed, some of the crowds of Dubliners who gathered to watch were so incensed that the Volunteers were glad of the protection afforded by their escort.

THOMAS MACDONAGH
talking to Éamonn Ceannt to give the message to surrender.

It took Nurse O'Farrell, accompanied by a priest, two days to bring the surrender order to all outposts. At Boland's Mill the orders had to be ratified by Thomas MacDonagh before Éamon de Valera would accept its veracity. At the College of Surgeons, Michael Mallin and Constance Markievicz surrendered reluctantly, while MacDonagh took the message in person to Éamonn Ceannt at the South Dublin Union.

3 May–3 August: The Executions and Their Consequences

On sending General John Maxwell to Ireland, British Prime Minister Herbert Asquith had given him full powers over the Irish administration.

A MAN LIES DEAD in the ruins of a cottage representing the shambles made of the attempt to create an Irish Republic. His hat labelled 'Sinn Féin Revolt' lies upended on the ground next to him, as does his rifle marked 'Made in Germany'.

This meant that Chief Secretary for Ireland, Augustine Birrell, and Lord Lieutenant of Ireland, Lord Wimbourne – who were much more in touch with the political sensitivity of the situation and the mood of the Irish people – had little power to stand against his decisions.

The brief to General Maxwell from the head of the British military, General Herbert Kitchener, was to '... take all such measures as may be ... necessary for the prompt suppression of the insurrection.' General Maxwell considered the insurgents' crimes as extremely serious: the conspiracy with Germany, the wartime enemy of Britain, the great toll of casualties, the property destroyed and the grave danger that the attempt might be repeated all informed his decision to seek capital punishment for all of the leaders.

COUNTING THE CASUALTIES

Not including those executed on General Maxwell's orders after the Rising, a total of 450 people died during the insurrection, with 2,614 wounded and nine missing. Of these, 230 of the dead were civilians, along with 64 insurgents out of a total force of 1,558. 116 British military were killed, 368 wounded and nine missing, while 16 policemen were killed and 29 wounded.

DUBLIN CASTLE
Scene of the imprisonment of many of the leaders of the 1916 Rising.

At Richmond Barracks, detectives and British military operated a court-martial selection, to identify the main Volunteers. They marked Clarke, MacDermott, MacDonagh, Ceannt and MacBride as leaders of the Rising and transferred them to Dublin Castle.

The rest of those arrested were either sent to internment camps in England or released. In total, 186 men were court-martialled, and one woman – Constance Markievizc. Unlike a public trial, the judges at the court martial were three British military officers, none of whom were required to have legal training. General Maxwell's further decision to have these trials in secret was later ruled to be illegal.

Of the 16 condemned to death, Roger Casement was the only one to have a public trial, largely because he was imprisoned in London. Tried at the Old Bailey, Casement was found guilty of treason and was hanged rather than being shot as a prisoner of war. General Maxwell assured Prime Minister Asquith that those to be executed would be either signatories of the Proclamation, commanding officers or known murderers, but Willie Pearse, Pádraig's younger brother, was also sentenced to death by virtue of the fact that he was Pearse's brother. Constance Markievicz was initially given a death sentence but this was then commuted to life imprisonment – 15 out of a total of 90 death sentences were commuted by General Maxwell himself.

Over a period of two weeks all seven signatories to the Proclamation, along with nine others, were shot at daybreak in a yard at Kilmainham Jail. De Valera was spared the death penalty because he was the last to be tried. By then, alarmed by the rising public sympathy for the rebels, Prime Minister Asquith had arrived in

Ireland to revoke General Maxwell's powers and call a halt to the executions. The executions were all carried out at Kilmainham Jail, apart from that of Thomas Kent, who was an agitator in Cork and was executed there, and Roger Casement, who was hanged at Pentonville in London.

EXECUTIONS

The 16 executions occurred on the following days: 3 May – Pádraig Pearse, Tom Clarke, Thomas MacDonagh; 4 May – Joseph Plunkett, Edward Daly, William Pearse, Michael O'Hanrahan; 5 May – John MacBride; 6 May – Éamonn Ceannt, Michael Mallin, Con Colbert, Seán Heuston; 9 May – Thomas Kent; 12 May – Seán MacDermott, James Connolly; 3 August – Roger Casement.

EASTER WEEK commemoration from 1933, the 17th anniversary of the Rising.

To a man, the leaders of the 1916 Rising showed great bravery in facing their fate. Pearse whistled as he walked from his cell to the yard and died holding a crucifix, and the unsinkable Tom Clarke refused the offer of a blindfold and faced the firing squad with his eyes open. The terminally ill Joseph Plunkett married his sweetheart, Grace Gifford, in the chapel hours before his death, and James Connolly remained dignified even though he was severely ill from gangrene and had to be tied to a chair to be shot. The firing squad comprised 12 men who fired at a point-blank range of 10 yards, supervised by an officer.

Easter Week Commemoration

P.H. Pearse.
T. Clarke.
S. McDermott.
J. Connolly.
J. M. Plunkett.
J. McBride.
E. Ceannt.
M. Mallin.
T. MacDonagh.
E. Daly.
C. Colbert.
J. Heuston.
R. Casement.
M. O'Hanrahan.
W. Pearse.
T. Kent.

1933

The executed rebels were buried in unmarked graves, some in quicklime at Arbour Hill, and some in Kilmainham and Cork, with the intention, General Maxwell said, of avoiding graves which would turn into focal points for martyrdom.

The long-lost remains of Thomas Kent were discovered at Cork Prison in June 2015 and identified by DNA analysis. He was buried with a full state funeral.

POSTER
showing the leaders of the 1916 Rising, including the 15 executed by the British.

Reactions of the Irish General Public

The secretiveness of the trials, the firing squads at dawn and the burial in unmarked graves had exactly the opposite effect to that intended.

BRITISH PRIME MINISTER HERBERT ASQUITH
leaving a barbed wire compound at Richmond Barracks, 13 May 1916.

John Dillon, the deputy leader of the Irish Parliamentary Party, accused the British establishment of '... doing everything possible to conceivably madden the Irish people ... you are letting loose a river of blood.'

Prime Minister Asquith had told General Maxwell that '... anything like a large number of executions would sow the seeds of lasting trouble in Ireland,' and indeed had tried to put a stop to them, but General Maxwell continued with the executions over nine days, only halting the proceedings when Asquith arrived in Dublin in person.

The Irish public were outraged – the rapid, secret trials and brutal executions of the gravely ill Connolly and similarly frail Plunkett just hours after his marriage, as well as those of Willie Pearse and the veteran John MacBride, added weight to the already established fury at the heavy-handedness of the British response to the 1916 Rising.

The tide of public opinion had already started turning after several atrocities were committed by British troops. The cover-up of the murder of well-known Dublin character Francis Sheehy-Skeffington,

JOSEPH PLUNKETT was imprisoned with his brothers George Oliver and Jack, pictured in a photograph published by *Le Mirroir*, in France. Joseph married Grace Gifford in prison and was executed seven hours later.

who had been arrested while trying to organise a citizens' police force to maintain law and order and contain looting, infuriated the public, as did the deaths on North King Street. The North King Street men had been casualties of Ned Daly's defeat of British troops at the Four Courts – maddened by their heavy losses, British soldiers dragged 15 civilian men from their homes and shot or bayoneted them.

From May onwards, the rebel leaders became martyrs and heroes, with commemorative postcards and photographs being issued. Money was raised for their families and, in a huge sea change, the

PRISONERS
Over 3,500 prisoners were taken by the British. This photograph from the French pictorial, *Le Mirroir*, shows a group of captured rebels being marched by British soldiers.

newspapers and the Catholic Church swayed in their opinion of the 1916 Rising, and began to support the rebels' cause.

The large-scale arrests also did not help matters – the authorities had incorrectly laid the blame for the Rising at the door of the Sinn Féin political party, and after the Rising had been put down approximately 3,430 men and 79 women were arrested for Sinn Féin membership, most of whom were innocent. Though 1,424 men were released without charge, the rest were deported to prisons and internment camps, further cementing Irish opinion against the British government. Of the 79 women arrested, all but seven were released and all within a relatively short period, the last in June 1917.

Support for John Redmond's Irish Parliamentary Party, which had campaigned for so long and so moderately for home rule all but disappeared – public opinion, swayed by the brutality of the British response, was now entrenched firmly in support of republicanism. Thus, a political vacuum opened up, into which stepped those veterans of the Rising who had been sufficiently junior in rank to avoid death. They built the political party Sinn Féin, which means 'ourselves alone', into a republican powerhouse. From 1917 they successfully waged a fierce campaign against the potential introduction of conscription into the British army, and in 1918, a mere two years after the Rising, they won by a landslide in the December 1918 General Election.

Reactions of the British General Public

Overall, the reaction of the British general public to the 1916 Rising was marked by feelings of anger, fear and confusion.

The reaction of the British public was similar to that of the Irish 'separation women', who were enraged at the perceived betrayal of their menfolk fighting Germany in the trenches. World War I marked a sea-change in British life, as it did across Europe, with the end of the Belle Époque, that period of time from 1871 to 1914 characterised by economic prosperity, peace and a flourishing of arts and culture. This world was eclipsed by the war and those who fought in it became known as the Lost Generation, referring both to the many dead lost in the trenches and all those soldiers who returned 'shell shocked', damaged for life by the trauma of the war.

AN IRISH HERO!
1 IRISHMAN DEFEATS 10 GERMANS.

SERGEANT MICHAEL O'LEARY, V.C.
· IRISH GUARDS ·
HAVE YOU NO WISH TO EMULATE THE SPLENDID BRAVERY OF YOUR FELLOW COUNTRYMAN?
JOIN AN IRISH REGIMENT TO-DAY

By 1916 the war had been grinding on for two years, and as well as the personal heartbreak for those with family and friends at the front, the unrelentingly heavy casualties and miserable conditions suffered by the 'Tommies' fighting in the trenches had been well-publicised by the British papers.

That Ireland would rebel while Britain was so vulnerable was shocking in itself, but to collude with their hated enemy in a conspiracy that could have tipped the balance of the entire war in their favour – the Rising was described by some British newspapers as a 'German plot' – was even more galling.

The other element that informed the reaction of the British public was ignorance of the history between Ireland and Britain and of how contemporary issues affected Ireland's population. Understandably, to those living in Southend in London or Aberdeen in Scotland, Ireland might have seemed an entirely alien population – connected, but remote. Yet, unlike Canada, the United States or Australia, Ireland was not a colony but a constituent part of the United Kingdom. Lack of knowledge and understanding of Irish issues and the motivation of the leaders of the 1916 Rising contributed to the mood of confusion and fear. Without this insight, the actions of the rebels were interpreted as aimed at the destruction of Britain rather than the freedom of Ireland.

1919: The Emergence of Sinn Féin

In the years following the 1916 Rising, Ireland was an increasingly divided society.

Unionism, a movement committed to keeping ties with Britain, remained a powerful influence, particularly in the north-east. However, between 1916 and 1919, the republican movement, those seeking complete independence, emerged as a major force. Initially the republicans had struggled in the months after the Rising. Several leading figures had been executed while the British authorities unleashed a wave of repression across the island. Thousands were interned without trial in prison camps, the most infamous of which was Frongoch in Wales. It was here that Michael Collins, a future leading republican, spent his months of imprisonment.

This wave of repression ultimately proved utterly counterproductive. Many of those interned after 1916 had little or no role in the events leading up to the

Rising. In the prison camps, however, they were influenced by the republican activists with whom they were incarcerated.

By May 1917 all prisoners had been released and most now committed themselves to struggling for an independent Ireland. They gravitated towards Sinn Féin, an organisation that had previously been very marginal in Irish society. The party reorganised itself, electing Éamon de Valera as leader.

Bolstered by thousands of activists who had been steeled by their experiences of the Rising and internment, Sinn Féin now set about achieving full independence for Ireland. This was resisted not only by the British authorities but also by the Ulster Unionist movement. Throughout 1917, the growth in support for Sinn Féin became apparent when they won three by-elections held that year. However, it was the final year of World War I, 1918, that saw Sinn Féin and

SOLE SURVIVOR
Éamon de Valera was sentenced to death, but was the only commandant of the Rising not to be executed. It is thought that his life was spared partly due to his US citizenship. He was released from life in prison in a June 1917 amnesty.

the republican movement transformed.

For most of the war, Ireland had been exempt from conscription to the British army. However, by 1918, after four years of bloody warfare, the army was facing a manpower crisis – there were no longer enough young men in Britain to send to war. Prime Minister Lloyd George decided to extend conscription to Ireland. This caused outrage.

ANTI-CONSCRIPTION rally in May 1918. Éamon de Valera spoke with John Dillon, the leader of the Irish Parliamentary Party, in Ballaghadareen, County Roscommon.

The idea of forcing men into a war from which many would not return was met with widespread opposition, and it was Sinn Féin that benefited most. Having always opposed the war and argued that home rule was not enough, they now experienced a surge of support. The key moment came when a general election was held in December 1918. Sinn Féin achieved a stunning victory over the unionists and the Irish Parliamentary Party, which supported home rule, winning 73 of the 105 Irish seats in Westminster. The main unionist party won 22 seats, predominantly in the north-east, while the Irish Parliamentary Party vote collapsed to a mere six seats.

CONSCRIPTION

The British move to compulsory conscription came due to deadly German offensives in March 1918. This raised the age limit to 50 and ended Irish exemption.

1919: The First Dáil Meets

After their resounding victory in the 1918 general election, Sinn Féin were by far the largest political force in Ireland.

Committed to establishing an independent Ireland, they immediately took steps to put this into place.

Elected Irish MPs usually sat in the parliament at Westminster in London, but Sinn Féin refused to take their seats. Instead, they established their own parliament in Dublin. Invitations were sent to all those who had won seats in Ireland, including unionists.

MEMBERS of the First Dáil (1919), at the Mansion House, Dublin.

On 21 January 1919 the first Irish parliament, known as the Dáil, met in the Mansion House in Dublin, the residence of the city's Lord Mayor.

Only members of Sinn Féin attended the first meeting of the First Dáil as Ireland took its first steps towards independence. Those present reasserted Ireland's right to self-determination. As the legitimate government of the island, they established institutions of a new state. A provisional constitution was agreed while their vision for society was published in a document called The Democratic Programme. At that historic first meeting they also appealed to the 'free nations' of the world to support Ireland's bid for independence.

CATHAL BRUGHA
in a painting by John F. Kelly, now hanging in Leinster House alongside portraits of Éamon de Valera and other Irish leaders.

POLICE NOTICE.

£1000 REWARD

WANTED FOR MURDER IN IRELAND.

DANIEL BREEN

(calls himself Commandant of the Third Tipperary Brigade).

Age 27, 5 feet 7 inches in height, bronzed complexion, dark hair (long in front), grey eyes, short cocked nose, stout build, weight about 12 stone, clean shaven; sulky bulldog appearance; looks rather like a blacksmith coming from work; wears cap pulled well down over face.

The above reward will be paid by the Irish Authorities, to any person not in the Public Service who may give information resulting in his arrest.

Information to be given at any Police Station.

The republican leader Cathal Brugha presided over the meeting as Éamon de Valera was still imprisoned in Lincoln Jail in England. Several others were appointed to key positions, notably Michael Collins, an emerging figure, who was appointed Minister for Finance. In the following months this government-in-waiting slowly began to take over aspects of day-to-day life in many areas of Ireland. This was best seen in the judicial arena, where the Dáil established its own legal system, operating in parallel to the British system. While the meeting of the First Dáil was a deeply significant historical event, on that same day another event took place that was of no less import.

As Sinn Féin had emerged in the years after 1916, so too had the Irish Republican Army (IRA). Committed to fighting for the Irish Republic, its actions prior to 1919 were limited. This changed, coincidentally, as the First Dáil was meeting in Dublin. At Soloheadbeg in rural Tipperary, a group of republican volunteers, led by Seán Hogan, Seán Treacy and Dan Breen, attacked a convoy of explosives in transit to a local quarry. Two policemen escorting the convoy were killed. The British response was swift and decisive. The entire region was declared a Special Military Area, where many freedoms were curtailed. Given what followed, these shots are regarded as the first fired in the Irish War of Independence.

1919: The War of Independence Begins

The shots fired by the IRA at Soloheadbeg in South Tipperary in January 1919 opened the Irish War of Independence.

While the Dáil ratcheted up political pressure on the British government, attacks on British garrisons across Ireland increased in the following months.

ÉAMON DE VALERA taking the salute of Sinn Féiners as they march past in 1919.

The war that raged in Ireland between 1919 and 1921 was not a conventional conflict. The IRA, aware of their disadvantage against the far better equipped and trained British army, avoided open conflict and

large-scale battles. Ambushes and night attacks on isolated garrisons were the preferred and most effective tactics. The British authorities responded with an increasingly brutal war, which all too often was waged against the wider population. This served to increase opposition to the army and police.

This was seen in Limerick when the area was declared a Special Military Area, in which travel was severely restricted. Local trade unions responded by declaring a general strike. They even went as far as taking over control of the city for over a week and issuing their own currency.

As the British government lost control of the country, they responded to the insurgents with increasing violence and repression. In September 1919 the Dáil was declared illegal. Many of its members were heavily involved in the war. As IRA Director of Intelligence, Michael Collins was responsible for planning the assassination of several high profile British military figures in Dublin.

THE LIMERICK SOVIET was a self-declared soviet that existed from 15 to 27 April 1919 in County Limerick. The Limerick Soviet ran the city for the period, printed its own money and organised the distribution of food.

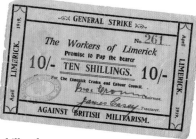

The later months of 1919 saw the conflict escalate in intensity. In what later became an official policy, the British army increasingly burned homes, farms and, in some cases, even towns that they suspected of supporting republicans. As the British army failed to grapple with the situation, two paramilitary organisations were sent to Ireland to support the army in the early months of 1920. The most notorious of these became known as the Black and Tans, named after their mismatched uniforms. Untrained and lacking discipline, their arrival heralded an increase in atrocities.

In April, after the IRA attacked and burned a police barracks in County Limerick, the Black and Tans responded by rampaging through nearby Limerick city. This was the first of several such attacks. Before the year was out, towns in Clare, Meath, Sligo, Longford, Dublin and Kerry were burned. This served to increase popular antipathy towards the British establishment in Ireland.

In the final months of 1920 the war intensified still further. In October three IRA prisoners died on hunger strike, including Terence McSwiney, Lord Mayor of Cork. A week later an 18-year-old republican student, Kevin Barry, was hanged in Mountjoy Jail, an execution that caused particular outrage in Dublin.

This was followed by an event that became known as Bloody Sunday, when the British army, in response to a series of assassinations in Dublin, randomly fired into a crowd at a Gaelic football match at Croke Park killing 14 people, including one player.

As 1920 drew to a close, 17 British soldiers were killed by the IRA in one of the most lethal ambushes of the war at Kilmichael in County Cork. As the violence increased, it became clear that the power of the British administration in Ireland was in crisis and martial law was declared across the south-west.

THE BRITISH, led by the Auxiliaries, a paramilitary unit of the RIC, and supported by the Black and Tans, raided Croke Park and started firing five minutes after the match began.

1920: The Act for the Partition of Ireland Passed

Facing an increasing crisis in Ireland, the British government of David Lloyd George decided to challenge the republican movement politically as well as militarily.

A STAMP
issued in support of home rule.

Prior to World War I the major demand among nationalists in Ireland had been home rule. This would have seen Ireland ruled by a parliament in Dublin while remaining within the British Empire. The republican movement, however, continued to argue that this was not enough and demanded full independence.

In an effort to drain their support, Prime Minister Lloyd George attempted to introduce home rule with the Government of Ireland Act, but this proved to be deeply controversial. To placate the unionists, who had long feared being ruled by a nationalist government in Dublin, Ireland was partitioned. Two parliaments, one in Belfast and one in Dublin, were to be established. The Belfast parliament would govern the six north-eastern counties of Ireland – the heartland of unionism. Meanwhile, the Dublin parliament was to have sway over the remaining 26 counties. Ireland would be split into two jurisdictions for the first time.

By June 1921 the Belfast parliament had been established. However, this was a deeply sectarian institution. Comprised predominantly of unionists, it discriminated heavily against nationalist communities across the six counties. The establishment of the Dublin parliament to administer home rule across the remaining 26 counties, much of which territory was under martial law, proved to be an impossible task. Nevertheless, an election was called for June 1921.

ROBINSON AND CLEAVER DEPARTMENT STORE IN BELFAST, decorated for the state opening of the first Northern Ireland parliament. 22 June 1921.

THIS POSTER
states the arguments espoused by pro-Treaty adherents such as Michael Collins and Arthur Griffith, signatories to the Anglo-Irish Treaty in London on 6 December 1921.

The result of the election showed that British rule was becoming unworkable in parts of Ireland. Amid accusations of intimidation, all the Sinn Féin MPs who had won seats in the general election of 1918 stood unopposed. As there were no other candidates, the election was a formality, and Sinn Féin took all the seats. As they had after the 1918 election, Sinn Fein representatives refused to recognise British institutions, even a parliament sitting in Dublin.

Lloyd George's political attempt to undermine the republican movement failed and the war continued unabated. In May 1921, in one of the biggest actions of the entire conflict, several hundred IRA volunteers seized the Custom House, a prominent landmark in Dublin. The departure from the tactics of guerrilla warfare resulted in heavy casualties.

As the summer of 1921 wore on, IRA leaders were increasingly aware that they would not be able to continue the conflict indefinitely. As in England, a society emerging from the horrors of war had little stomach for another long conflict. A truce was called. This was followed by face-to-face negotiations between the British government and representatives of the Irish republican movement in London. De Valera, President of Sinn Féin, did not attend. He appointed Arthur Griffith and Michael Collins to lead a delegation to negotiate a treaty with a British team, which included Lloyd George and Winston Churchill.

CUSTOM HOUSE
The fire brigade arrive to put out the fire at the Custom House in May 1921.

1921: The Anglo-Irish Treaty Signed

Throughout November and December 1921, tense negotiations took place between the Irish and British delegations in Downing Street, London.

THE SIGNING of the Anglo-Irish Treaty in London in 1921.

Finally, on 6 December, a document known as the Anglo-Irish Treaty was agreed by both sides. This was then taken to Ireland for ratification.

It was immediately clear that the document would be controversial. Michael Collins said he was in effect signing his own death warrant when he put his name to the treaty.

While the terms of the Anglo-Irish Treaty would see an end to the war in Ireland and a withdrawal of most British troops, it fell far short of the aims

of the republican movement. Ireland was not to become a fully independent country. Instead the new Irish Free State would remain part of the British Commonwealth, which meant that Irish political representatives would still have to take an oath of allegiance to the British monarch. Even more controversially, Ireland was to remain partitioned. The six north-eastern counties that had been governed by the Belfast parliament since 1920 would remain part of the United Kingdom.

THE PARTITION OF IRELAND IS A CRIME AGAINST INTERNATIONAL JUSTICE

IT **MUST** BE *RIGHTED*

ULSTER

▦▦▦ PARTITION BOUNDARY
■■■ MAJORITY AGAINST PARTITION
▨▨▨ 25% TO 50% AGAINST PARTITION
■■■ MAJORITY FOR PARTITION

ANTI-PARTITION PROPAGANDA
label showing the proportion in Ulster in favour of partition at the time.

With the delegates back in Dublin, the depth of division within the republican movement over the Anglo-Irish Treaty was revealed. De Valera opposed ratification of the document and the cabinet passed it by only a single vote.

In January 1922 the Treaty was discussed by the Dáil. The debates were stormy. Michael Collins told the assembly that Lloyd George had threatened an all-out war in Ireland if the Treaty were rejected. After nine days of debate, it was ratified by a narrow margin of 64 to 57 votes. De Valera resigned as President and the republican movement became increasingly divided.

When the pro-Treaty politicians proceeded to establish what became known as the Irish Free State, they faced an even thornier problem – the IRA. Many of its members, men who had fought in the War of Independence, were deeply unhappy with the terms. They held a convention in Dublin in March 1922 and categorically rejected the Treaty, with a two-thirds majority voting against.

The IRA now elected their own executive to which they pledged their allegiance, in effect rejecting the authority of the Dáil. Meanwhile, Michael Collins and the leaders of the new Irish Free State established their own army. Ireland was increasingly divided and heading towards a civil war. The following months saw tensions rise.

In April, armed anti-Treaty republicans, led by the IRA Director of Engineering, Rory O'Connor, occupied the Four Courts, a complex of buildings that dominated the north quays in Dublin. In May Kilkenny Castle was occupied by anti-Treaty republicans.

This led to a shoot-out with the new Free State army.

Against the background of these tensions elections were held that were, in many respects, a referendum on the treaty. Led by Michael Collins, pro-Treaty republicans secured 58 seats, while the anti-Treaty candidates secured only 36. The pro-Treaty Labour Party won 17 seats.

Heartened by this, Michael Collins ordered Free State forces to move against the republicans in the Four Courts complex in Dublin. When they refused to leave, the building was shelled. The Irish Civil War, which had been looming for months, had begun.

THE DOME OF THE FOUR COURTS
ablaze during the battle, 30 June 1922.

1922: The Death of Michael Collins

MICHAEL COLLINS was killed in an ambush by anti-Treaty forces.

The government shelling of the Four Courts made a wider conflict inevitable.

The anti-Treaty republicans were in a poor position to mount an effective opposition to the new Irish Free State.

While they initially outnumbered the fledgling Free State army, they lacked arms and cohesion. They were also divided on what strategy to adopt. Most, if not all, were desperate to avoid open conflict with their former comrades.

The Free State army was increasingly heavily armed and showed itself to be far more ruthless in its willingness to go on the offensive.

In the initial weeks the anti-Treaty forces secured much of the territory in the south and west, while the newly elected government continued to recruit troops. In the late summer the Free State army went on the offensive. The anti-Treaty forces lacked unity and were relatively poorly armed, and they soon lost the major towns under their control. In their key base of Munster, the cities of Cork, Limerick and Waterford were taken by the Free State army with relative ease.

By August the commander of the anti-Treaty forces, Liam Lynch, had ordered his troops to stop trying to hold towns, which was becoming an increasingly pointless strategy. They returned to the guerrilla tactics they had used so efficiently in the War of Independence. A few weeks later one such ambush claimed the most famous casualty of the war, when Michael Collins was assassinated while travelling through West Cork.

The loss of the 32-year-old

LIAM LYNCH
anti-Treaty leader, who was shot in County Waterford.

Collins was a major blow, but the Free State army nevertheless continued the war. The following months were marked by several atrocities. The new government, now led by W.T. Cosgrave, ordered the extra-judicial killings of several prisoners in retribution for the assassination of a government politician. Worse was to follow.

In Ballyseedy, County Kerry, Free State forces strapped several republican prisoners to a land mine on a bridge, which was then detonated. The story only emerged because one man had been blown clear of the bridge in the explosion and survived. Meanwhile, anti-Treaty forces responded by attacking Cosgrave's home and killing his elderly uncle.

However, the outcome of the Civil War had not been in doubt since the summer of 1922. Slowly but surely the better armed and organised Irish Free State army ground down their opponents. In April 1923 the anti-Treaty leader Liam Lynch was shot in County Waterford and died a few hours later from his wounds.

He was replaced as Chief of Staff by Frank Aiken, who ordered his troops to dump their arms and stop the conflict. The Civil War had come to an end. However, while the IRA implicitly acknowledged defeat, they did not disband and saw this as an opportunity to survive to fight another day.

GOVERNMENT TROOPS
escorting a prisoner in 1923 in Ballyseedy.

1922: The Irish Free State is Established

During the Civil War the pro-Treaty members of Sinn Féin, unable to rely on the party for support, formed their own political party, which they called Cumann na nGaedheal.

W.T. COSGRAVE
William Thomas Cosgrave (1880–1965), first President of the Executive Council of the Irish Free State.

Having defeated the anti-Treaty forces in the Civil War, Cumann na nGaedheal, led by W.T. Cosgrave, set about entrenching their position in wider Irish society. They represented business and large farming interests and although they had emerged during a revolutionary period, they were deeply conservative. Indeed, one of the most prominent figures in this ruling party, Kevin O'Higgins, famously described himself as one of 'the most conservative-minded revolutionaries that ever put through a successful revolution'. The party felt that since 1916 Ireland had seen too much change.

During these years trade unions had grown significantly. There had been numerous general strikes and widespread demands for better conditions for

workers. The revolutionary years had also seen great advances for women. In 1918 Ireland elected the first female MP to the House of Commons when Constance Markievicz, a prominent member of Sinn Féin, won a seat in Dublin. In the years after the Civil War, Cumann na nGaedheal attempted to reverse many of these advances.

1924 saw violent attacks on farm labourers who went on strike, while several attempts were made to exclude women from public life. Most notably, Kevin O'Higgins attempted to exclude them entirely from jury duty. These conservative attitudes also reflected

PHOTOGRAPH
of the Irish Free State Constitution Committee, 1922.

THE SITE OF Kevin O'Higgins' murder in Booterstown, July 1927.

the growing power of the Catholic Church in post-independence Ireland. Most of the Cumann na nGaedheal leaders were deeply devout Catholics and the position of the Church strengthened enormously in the years following the establishment of the Irish Free State.

Such conservatism ensured that the early years of independence were very difficult for many people in Ireland. The reality of independence fell far short of the society set out in the 1916 Proclamation and the Democratic Programme of the First Dáil. To make matters worse, the mid-1920s were very difficult years economically. Repeated wet weather and poor harvests resulted in severe food and fuel shortages. Emigration soared and many fell into destitution.

While the Civil War had come to an end in 1923, political violence did not. The IRA had dumped their arms in 1923 but they did not disband. In July 1927 they shot and killed Kevin O'Higgins on his way to Mass. He was targeted as he had been responsible for the execution of several anti-Treaty prisoners during the Civil War.

POVERTY was endemic in much of Ireland.

Meanwhile, in the north-eastern six counties of the island, which remained part of the United Kingdom, life was little better. While the Civil War divided the republican movement in the south, it was somewhat less divisive in these counties, as most republicans opposed the Treaty. They continued to fight the authorities in Belfast until late 1922. This conflict claimed over 460 lives in Belfast alone. While the IRA in the six counties was more or less defeated by the end of 1922, the years that followed were marked by frequent sectarian violence and poverty.

1930s: Fianna Fáil and Éamon de Valera

ELECTION POSTER
from Cumann na nGaedheal, making much of an alleged communist threat.

During the early 1920s, the one-time republican leader Éamon de Valera became an increasingly marginalised figure.

Despite initially leading the opposition to the Treaty, he played little active role during the Civil War. In the following years, he and the remaining members of Sinn Féin (the pro-Treaty politicians had left to form Cumann na nGaedheal) grew increasingly irrelevant. Viewing the Dáil as an illegitimate institution, they refused to take their seats, leaving de Valera in a political wilderness.

By the mid-1920s, he was one of several who began to realise that they would never win widespread support unless they took their seats. In 1926 he introduced a motion at a Sinn Féin gathering advocating that they drop their abstentionist policy. This was resisted by many hardline republicans in Sinn Féin and the motion was defeated.

De Valera, unwilling to sit on the sidelines of Irish politics any longer, resigned his membership of Sinn Féin. Along with several other prominent like-minded republicans he set up a new party, one which would dominate Irish politics for the following eight decades. The new party was called Fianna Fáil – the soldiers of destiny.

Fianna Fáil remained opposed to the Treaty, but was now willing to engage with the institutions of the Free State. They pitched themselves to small farmers and workers and gained substantial support. In the late 1920s their policy of economic self-sufficiency had wide appeal.

Their first major test came when a general election was called in 1927. Fianna Fáil polled exceedingly well, taking 43 seats and almost

FIANNA FÁIL, led by Éamon de Valera, won the election of 1932.

obliterating Sinn Féin. In the aftermath of the election it was not possible to form a coalition and another election was called in the autumn of 1927. Cumannn na nGaedheal were returned to power, but Fianna Fáil increased their vote, taking several seats from the Labour Party.

Over the next five years Fianna Fáil continued to grow in popularity while the ruling Cumann na nGaedheal floundered. The early 1930s were marked by a severe global recession, and when an election was called in 1932, it seemed that de Valera's moment had arrived. When the votes were tallied, Fianna Fáil had scored a stunning electoral victory that carried them into government. They took 72 seats in comparison to the 57 secured by their rivals, Cumann na nGaedheal.

Fianna Fáil's first term of office in Ireland was marked by an increasingly fractious relationship with the United Kingdom. Following their policy of self-sufficiency, de Valera began what became known as the Economic War, imposing high taxes on imported goods from the UK. The British government responded with similar taxes on goods from Ireland. This resulted in increased hardship for the Irish people, and by 1935 de Valera began to ease the policy and the Economic War came to an end in 1938. However, the government's greatest influence was on legislation. In 1937 they drafted a new constitution for Ireland.

1937: The Constitution of Ireland

On coming to power in 1932, Éamon de Valera and Fianna Fáil were keen to transform the Irish Free State into an independent republic.

DOUGLAS HYDE
Portrait of Douglas Hyde, first President of Ireland (1860-1949), by John Butler Yeats.

Under the terms of the Anglo-Irish Treaty of 1921, the Free State still maintained political links to the United Kingdom, while Irish members of parliament still took an oath of allegiance to the British monarch as head of state.

Where possible they broke these political links through acts of parliament. For example, the hated oath of allegiance was removed. In 1937 the changes were enshrined in a new constitution. Éamon de Valera oversaw the drafting of this constitution with legal scholars and, perhaps most controversially, with the Catholic theologian and future archbishop of Dublin, John Charles McQuaid.

The new constitution removed references to Britain wherever possible. The name of the country was changed from the Irish Free State to Ireland. Articles 2 and 3 also reflected anti-Treaty sentiment in Fianna Fáil, claiming sovereignty over the entire island of Ireland.

Provisions were also made for a new position of president as head of state, undermining the status of the British monarch. The new constitution was passed by the Dáil in June 1937 and subsequently put to a referendum the following July. The constitution passed by margin of 685,105 to 526,945 votes and came into effect on 29 December 1937. The following summer Douglas Hyde, a prominent scholar, became Ireland's first president.

Whilst the architects of the new constitution were keen to increase Ireland's independence from Britain, the document also reflected the rising power of the Catholic Church in Ireland. John Charles McQuaid had enormous influence over the social and religious policy in the text. While the constitution enshrined the freedom to worship for all religions, it noted the 'special position' of the Catholic Church. It recognised the family as the 'natural primary and fundamental unit-group of society'. To reinforce this primacy, divorce was banned. This provision also had a major influence on the role of women in society. They were primarily viewed as mothers and wives and attempts were made to restrict their ability to work outside the home.

After the ratification of the 1937 Constitution, the 26 southern counties occupied an ambiguous position. Officially they were not yet an independent republic. Technically there were two heads of state, the king of England and, after 1937, the president of Ireland. In 1949 this ambiguity was finally rectified when Taoiseach John A. Costello declared the 26 southern counties of Ireland an independent republic. All references to Britain in the legal framework of the state were removed.

JOHN A. COSTELLO
Taoiseach of Ireland, 1948-51 and 1954-7.

IRELAND'S RIGHT TO UNITY

THE MAP

There is a majority of 80 per cent. in the whole of Ireland for unity. A minority opposition to national freedom was made the excuse by Britain, who organised and sustained it, for the partition of Ireland in 1920. That opposition comes mainly from an area, marked orange on the map, which is roughly within a 30 miles radius of Belfast. The area is just over one-third of the partitioned territory and is only one-sixteenth of Ireland. Outside it, there is a continuous block from the extreme north with the extreme south to the extreme north with a majority for unity. Within the partitioned area itself there is a majority in almost two-thirds of the territory for re-union with the rest of Ireland.

ULSTER

BELFAST

CONNACHT

GALWAY

DUBLIN

LEINSTER

MUNSTER

CORK

The case stated by the All-Party
Anti-Partition Conference
Mansion House, Dublin, Ireland

- - - - - - - - - - - - - -
British imposed Border

IRELAND'S RIGHT TO UNITY

The case stated by the All-Party Anti-Partition Conference, Mansion House, Dublin, 1949.

1973: Ireland Joins the EEC

By 1949 the conservative revolutionaries who had brought the Republic of Ireland into being had achieved most of their goals.

THE ANNIE MOORE MEMORIAL

Statue of Annie Moore and her two brothers in Cobh. Annie was the first immigrant to the United States to pass through the Ellis Island facility in New York Harbour. Emigration to the United States continued throughout the 20th century.

They had finally succeeded in establishing an Irish republic, albeit one that did not include the six north-eastern counties of Ireland.

However, by the 1950s the country was facing a major crisis. Successive governments had failed to develop industry, and one of the key sectors of the economy – small farms – was in irreversible decline.

By the 1950s economic depression was ravaging Ireland; that decade is regarded as one of the worst in modern Irish history. Emigration, which had continued steadily since the famine of the 1840s, reached epic proportions. Between 1950 and 1960, around half a million people, mostly young, left Ireland seeking employment. Most travelled to England but others crossed the Atlantic to the United States. Ireland endured the ignominy of being one of only two countries in Europe to witness a fall in population in that decade, the other being East Germany.

Increasingly, Ireland's political leaders saw that the only viable option for the country was to forge closer links with Europe. In the aftermath of World War II, several European countries had developed close economic ties, resulting in the formation of the European Economic Community (forerunner to the EU) in 1957. Access to the large markets available in Europe made membership highly desirable for Ireland. However, attempts to join the EEC were by no means straightforward. Ireland's neutrality during World War II raised doubts, while the country's flagging economy offered little benefit.

1 EANAIR, 1973

E E C

CLÚDACH CHÉAD LAE

PART OF THE
design from an Irish First Day Cover celebrating accession to the EEC in 1973.

An initial attempt to join in 1961 was almost immediately rebuffed. In the following years new economic strategies saw the economy in Ireland grow as trade barriers were removed. Nevertheless, later attempts in 1962 and 1967 were blocked by France.

Finally, in 1972 Ireland successfully applied for membership. A referendum was held in May 1972 and membership was overwhelmingly accepted by the electorate, with over 83 per cent voting yes.

CIVIL RIGHTS ASSOCIATION demonstration in Norhern Ireland, where the army made many arrests.

This led to significant changes. The EEC's Common Agricultural Policy (CAP) brought an increase in prices for farm produce, while significant amounts of capital were made available for infrastructural projects. This helped to stem the flow of emigration; the 1970s even saw a slight reversal of the trend. However, while the Republic of Ireland was turning a corner, lingering tensions in the six counties of Ulster exploded violently.

1970s: Northern Ireland and the Troubles

In the 1950s the Republic's economy flagged and poverty and emigration soared. Meanwhile a very different, divided and unequal society emerged in Northern Ireland.

Unionists who sought to maintain closer links with the United Kingdom dominated Northern Ireland. The nationalist population in the region was heavily discriminated against. Political differences largely overlapped the religious divide, with nationalists by and large tending to be Catholic while unionists were predominantly Protestant. This imbued class tensions with religious sectarianism, creating an explosive mix.

By the early 1960s, although the nationalist community comprised 40 per cent of the population, they were largely excluded from political life. Electoral constituencies were

THE SHANKILL ROAD, BELFAST, during the Troubles, around 1970.

gerrymandered – constituency boundaries were drawn in a way that maximised unionist votes while minimising those of nationalists. Other forms of discrimination saw high levels of unemployment among nationalists. The authorities had wide-ranging powers of arrest and detention without charge. Four decades of political alienation, poverty and harassment from the authorities had filled reservoirs of resentment in the nationalist community by the 1960s. In 1968, inspired by the civil rights movement in the United States, nationalists began to organise for equal rights.

FIGHTING flared on the streets with running battles between the police and nationalists.

The first major flashpoint took place in Derry in 1969 in an event subsequently dubbed the Battle of the Bogside. After a controversial march by the unionist Orange Order, the police attacked nationalist communities as they attempted to defend themselves. The situation escalated into a minor revolt lasting several days. This was followed by an

increasing wave of repression and the situation began to spiral out of control. The republican movement, which had remained active on a low level, now began to re-emerge and took a leading role. While both Sinn Féin and the IRA split over tactics in 1969, one faction – the Provisional IRA, which advocated a more aggressive militaristic strategy – emerged as a powerful force by the early 1970s. The push for civil rights now increasingly turned into a violent struggle for a united Ireland, a struggle that was euphemistically called 'the Troubles'.

1971–2 was a decisive period. In August 1971 the British army shot and killed ten people in a major operation against the republican movement in Ballymurphy, West Belfast. The following January the British army shot 26 people at a civil rights demonstration in the Bogside of Derry. Fourteen died from their injuries. This massacre, known as Bloody Sunday, was a watershed moment. It provoked outrage across Ireland. The British Embassy in Dublin was burned during a demonstration and many young men and women joined republican paramilitaries, believing there was no peaceful solution available.

In the years that followed, the increasing number of IRA attacks on the British army were countered with draconian measures. As the death toll reached 1,000 people in 1974, it seemed impossible to call a halt to the escalating conflict. While the intensity of the Troubles began to ebb towards the late 1970s, the deaths of ten republican prisoners on hunger strike in 1981 transformed the IRA. Again, hundreds flocked to the organisation. All through the 1980s, the Troubles continued with car bombings and assassinations. However, by the mid-1990s, with the death toll approaching 3,500, it was clear that the conflict was approaching a stalemate. As all sides sought an end to the Troubles, some form of compromise was inevitable.

FR EDWARD DALY helps to escort a wounded man to safety on Bloody Sunday.

1998: The Good Friday Agreement

After nearly 30 years of conflict in Northern Ireland, there were increasing demands for peace by the mid-1990s.

PEACE TALKS
with Tony Blair, Martin McGuinness, David Trimble, John Hume, Bill Clinton, Ian Paisley, Gerry Adams and Bertie Ahern.

Tentative discussions began, but proved to be highly complex. All sides had suffered greatly and had endured personal tragedies. The first major breakthrough came when the IRA announced a ceasefire in 1994. In the following 17 months, negotiations took place, while the US government increasingly put pressure on all parties to end the conflict. This culminated in a visit from US President Bill Clinton to Belfast in 1995. However, these early attempts failed and the IRA ended its ceasefire on 9 February

1996. Later that day a huge IRA bomb exploded in London's Canary Wharf, killing two people and causing over a hundred million pounds of damage.

In the following months, attempts to bring about a permanent end to the war continued. However, in June 1996 an IRA bomb devastated central Manchester, while the following summer saw sectarian tensions flare over controversial Orange Order marches through nationalist communities in Northern Ireland. Nevertheless, 1998 brought a new IRA ceasefire.

AN ORANGE ORDER MARCH in Northern Ireland.

This was followed by months of hectic negotiations. All sides, including the British and Irish governments, representatives of the nationalist and unionist communities, as well as international figures debated the key points. On Good Friday 1998, a lasting settlement was reached after lengthy talks in Belfast.

The agreement, officially titled the Belfast Agreement, became widely known as the Good Friday Agreement. It mapped out a framework for permanent peace with a power-sharing government established in Belfast, designed to ensure that neither community could dominate the other as the unionists had been doing. The British government agreed to a full investigation into the Bloody Sunday massacre and to demilitarise Northern Ireland. The Irish government agreed to hold a referendum on Articles 2 and 3 of the constitution, which asserted sovereignty over the 32 counties (the referendum was passed). Meanwhile, most paramilitary organisations agreed to decommission their weapons, while prisoners serving sentences relating to the conflict were to be released.

While this agreement brought the major players in the conflict to peace, the

THE MEMORIAL GARDEN
in Omagh, with a mirror for each of those who died in the Omagh bombing, photographed by Kenneth Allen.

following years were fraught with difficulty. Minority factions within the republican movement did not believe the Belfast Agreement went far enough. Scarcely a few months after Good Friday 1998 a splinter group called the Real IRA detonated a bomb in Omagh, killing 29 people. This attempt to derail the process failed and in the following years much of the agreement came into force.

MURAL CELEBRATING workers at Harland & Wolff, Belfast, and the building of the *Titanic*. Belfast has traditionally been a centre for shipbuilding, but this sector declined in the 20th century.

Despite carrying out one of the largest bank robberies in the country's history in 2004, in 2005 the IRA finally announced it had given up its armed campaign and was fully committed to peace. While the Belfast Agreement has brought about a far more peaceful and stable society in Northern Ireland, it has not been without problems. Economically the six counties of Northern Ireland have struggled to develop. Unemployment remains high and the global recession in 2008 had a profound effect on the economy.

2010s: Modern Ireland

IRONIC POSTER
on a street in
Ireland, lampooning
the economic
downturn.

In the five decades since the beginning of the Troubles in the late 1960s, the Republic of Ireland has changed dramatically.

While the 1970s promised potential, the following decade proved to be a bleak period of very high unemployment and a return of emigration.

In the late 1990s, however, the economy began to grow rapidly. This economic growth – the so-called 'Celtic Tiger' – came to an abrupt end in 2008 when Ireland was heavily affected by the global recession. In the following five years, harsh austerity measures saw high levels of unemployment and a return of emigration rates not seen since the 1950s.

Whilst the economy has proved volatile, Ireland has witnessed massive social change in the last 20 years. The conservative attitudes that once dominated life are fast disappearing. Many of the traditional institutions of Irish society have lost influence. The power of the Catholic Church, in particular, has plummeted. Church attendance has fallen from 90 per cent in the 1950s to as little as 2 per cent in some areas. There are several reasons for this decline. First, Ireland has been rocked by several high profile child sex abuse cases since the early 1990s. Subsequent investigations revealed that the Catholic Church not only failed to halt the activities of paedophile priests but systematically moved them from parish to parish to protect them. Second, Ireland's

PARTS OF BELFAST are still divided by physical barriers: the peace wall of the Shankill Road in Belfast Northern Ireland, 2015

THE SPIRE OF DUBLIN, symbol of the modernisation and growing prosperity of Ireland, shown with the statue of James Larkin.

population is now highly educated, with a younger generation less willing to accept Church teachings without question as their grandparents had been inclined to.

Meanwhile the political landscape in Ireland has changed dramatically. Fianna Fáil, an organisation once referred to as the National Movement, which governed Ireland for 61 years in the period from 1932 to 2011, has gone into a decline. A series of scandals, which revealed some of the party's most senior figures to be corrupt, had little impact, but the widespread belief that the party was responsible for the economic collapse has seen their popularity plummet.

In these changing times Irish society has become increasingly socially liberal. In the 1990s, divorce was introduced and homosexual acts were decriminalised. Building on these advances, in 2015 Ireland became the first country in the world to vote in favour of same-sex unions by popular ballot. Since 1997 Ireland has witnessed large-scale immigration for the first time in its history. These changes have resulted in a more diverse, open and inclusive multicultural Ireland.

OPPOSING POSTERS in the 2015 campaign for equal marriage rights in Ireland.

Biographies

Michael Collins

James Connolly

James Craig

Éamon de Valera

William Gladstone

Maud Gonne

Arthur Griffith

James Larkin

David Lloyd George

Constance Markievicz

Seán O'Casey

Daniel O'Connell

Charles Stewart Parnell

Pádraig Pearse

John Redmond

W.B. Yeats

Michael Collins 1890–1922

Michael Collins was born on 16 October 1890 near Clonakilty in County Cork, the youngest of eight children in a farming family.

MICHAEL COLLINS joined the Irish Volunteers in 1916. He was killed in 1922 at Béal na Bláth by a ricochet bullet.

His upbringing in a fervently nationalist environment imbued him with a strong sense of patriotism. He finished school in 1906 at the age of 15, passed the civil service exam and took a job with the post office. Later that year he moved to London where he lived with his sister, had a job as a messenger for a firm of stockbrokers and studied law.

It was in London that he became involved in radical Irish nationalist politics. He joined Sinn Féin in 1908, the IRB the following year. In 1916 he returned to Ireland, taking up a part-time job with the Dublin firm of accountants Craig Gardiner. He immediately became involved in the planning of the Easter Rising, drilling volunteers and preparing weapons for the rebellion.

Although he fought alongside the other insurgents in the GPO and was arrested and imprisoned, he wasn't executed with the other leaders but was one of the vast majority of insurgents interned until the end of the year, then released.

Contingency plans had been set in place in the event of the failure of the 1916 Rising, and Collins was soon one of the leading figures in the drive towards independence led by Arthur Griffith, founder of Sinn Féin. By the end of 1917 Collins was on the executive of Sinn Féin and Éamon de Valera had replaced Arthur Griffith as president.

In the 1918 general election, Sinn Féin took 73 of 105 Irish seats, with Collins winning his seat for South Cork. The Sinn Féin deputies refused to take up their seats at Westminster, instead establishing a sovereign parliament – Dáil Éireann – in Dublin in January 1919. They declared Irish independence from Britain and elected de Valera as president of the Dáil. Collins was appointed Minister for Finance.

The first salvo in the Irish War of Independence was fired on the day of the first sitting of the Dáil, 21 January 1919, when the IRB ambushed two IRC officers at Soloheadbeg in County Tipperary. Although it had not sanctioned the attack, the Dáil's support for a military campaign became official.

A bitter and bloody campaign ended in a truce with Britain in July 1921.

De Valera appointed Collins to lead the Irish delegation at the peace conference in London. The Anglo-Irish Treaty of December 1921 established the Irish Free State, with six counties in the north remaining united with Britain. After days of acrimonious debate, the Treaty was passed by the Dáil with a very small majority, de Valera dissenting. Collins became Chairman and Finance Minister of the Provisional Government.

De Valera withdrew from the Dáil and the republican movement split into pro- and anti-Treaty factions, setting the stage for civil war. Collins orchestrated a successful campaign, but he was assassinated by anti-Treaty forces in an ambush at Béal na Bláth in County Cork on 22 August 1922.

James Connolly 1868–1916

James Connolly was born in Edinburgh to immigrant Irish parents on 5 June 1868.

JAMES CONNOLLY was brought up in poverty in Scotland, which gave him a lifelong interest in defending workers' rights.

He left school at the age of 10 or 11, to work with his brother at the *Edinburgh Evening News*, cleaning printing rollers. He joined the British Army at the age of 14 with his brother John, lying about his age. Stationed in Ireland for seven years, he became disaffected with the army. When his regiment was about to be transferred to India, he had himself discharged.

He married Lillie Reynolds, a Protestant, in April 1890, and went back to Edinburgh with his new wife. In 1895 he set up a cobbler's shop as a means of supporting his family, but he had no talent for mending shoes and the business failed. His involvement in the socialist movement was the priority in his life – he had been secretary of the Scottish Socialist Federation since 1892. When he was offered the job of full-time secretary to the Dublin Socialist Club in 1896, he moved to Dublin with his family. The club soon evolved into the Irish Socialist Republican Party (IRSP). Impatient with the party's slow progress, Connolly emigrated to the United States in 1903. While there, he joined all the main socialist organisations and founded the Irish Socialist Federation in 1907 in New York.

Connolly returned to Ireland in 1910, to act as James Larkin's right-hand man in the Irish Transport and General Workers' Union (ITGWU). During the 1913 Dublin Lockout he set up the Irish Citizen Army (ICA) to defend the striking workers against the brutal police response to the strike. The ICA soon moved its focus to the establishment of an independent socialist nation. Connolly founded the Irish Labour Party in 1912 and, had it not been for his participation in the 1916 Rising, this would have been his lasting political contribution to the new nation.

Because they were a non-socialist grouping with no focus on improving the economic situation of the Irish people, Connolly didn't take the Irish Volunteers seriously, believing that they would never do anything concrete towards achieving Irish independence. He threatened to send the ICA to fight against the British Empire, so the IRB leadership decided to meet with him to pre-empt such an action in advance of their own planned insurrection. When Tom Clarke and Pádraig Pearse met with Connolly in 1916, they agreed to combine their forces at Easter, appointing Connolly as Commandant of the Dublin Brigade of the Irish volunteers. This made him commander-in-chief of the 1916 Rising in all but name.

When the rebels surrendered, Connolly was arrested and sentenced to death. He had been mortally wounded during the fighting and had to be tied to a chair in order to be shot, on 12 May 1916. The execution of the other leaders of the rising had been controversial, both in Ireland and Britain, but the execution of a dying man seemed particularly brutal and the tide of public opinion turned sharply in support of the rebels.

There is a statue of Connolly outside Liberty Hall, Dublin, and one of Dublin's two main railway stations is named after him.

James Craig 1871–1940

James Craig, the first Prime Minister of Northern Ireland, was born in Belfast on 8 January 1871, the son of a whiskey millionaire.

JAMES CRAIG was a staunch unionist, serving as Prime Minister of Northern Ireland.

He was sent to public school in Scotland but didn't attend university, and started his working life at the age of 17 in a firm of stockbrokers, learning the trade from the ground up. On his return to Belfast he set up his own stockbroking establishment.

When the Boer War started in October 1899, Craig enlisted in the British Army. He received a commission and was a popular officer. He was sent home in 1901, suffering from dysentery – by the time he had recovered, the war was over. His father had died in 1900, leaving his son a large bequest that meant he didn't have to work for a living. In 1905 he met and married Cecil Mary Nowell Dering Tupper. Looking for more excitement than was offered by a career as a stockbroker, he decided to enter politics and was elected as the Ulster Unionist MP for East Down in 1906. He served as Parliamentary Secretary in two government departments, Pensions and the Admiralty. In the first decade of the 20th century,

Westminster was on course, after more than a century of campaigning by Irish MPs, to grant home rule to Ireland. As a staunch Protestant, unionist and member of the Orange Order, Craig was vehemently opposed to it and he rallied the Ulster Unionists, setting up and arming the Ulster Volunteers. In September 1912, almost 500,000 people signed the Ulster Covenant in an attempt to protect their way of life as Protestants in Northern Ireland.

Under the Government of Ireland Act 1920, Ireland was partitioned into the six counties of Northern Ireland and the 26 counties of the south. Each territory was to have its own home rule parliament. However, events took on a new momentum after the 1916 Rising when it became clear that home rule was no longer a viable option for the 26 counties; they were instead conferred with dominion status as the Irish Free State in 1922.

Northern Ireland's new home rule parliament was at Stormont, and the Lord Lieutenant of Ireland appointed Craig Prime Minister of Northern Ireland. Under his leadership, government appointments were made on a sectarian basis, frequently justified by Craig, who believed that all Catholics were subversives and that the state had to be protected from them. Throughout his long premiership, Craig became less and less engaged with Westminster and failed to advocate for safeguards for Northern Ireland's industrial sector when negotiations in 1938 brought a conclusion to the Economic War between the newly created Republic of Ireland and Britain.

In 1918 Craig was made a baronet. In 1927 he was created Viscount Craigavon of Stormont. He died in office on 24 November 1940, while serving his fifth term as Prime Minister of Northern Ireland.

Éamon de Valera **1882–1975**

Born on 14 October 1882 in New York, Éamon de Valera was brought to Limerick by Irish relatives when he was two years old, after the death of his father.

ÉAMON DE VALERA became the first Taoiseach of the Dáil in 1937, as leader of Fianna Fáil.

He was educated at Blackrock College, Dublin, and became a maths teacher. In 1910 he married Sinéad Flanagan, and they had five children, born between 1910 and 1918.

In 1913 de Valera joined the Irish Volunteers. During the 1916 Rising he had charge of the occupation of Boland's Mill on Grand Canal Street in Dublin. After the surrender he was sentenced to death, but the sentence was commuted to penal servitude for life. (He was an American citizen and Britain was campaigning very hard to persuade the United States to take up arms in World War I.) He was imprisoned in England, but was released in 1917 under the general amnesty.

In 1917 he was elected president of Sinn Féin, which went on to a landslide victory in the 1918 elections. Their plans to establish a national government had to go ahead without de Valera, who was rearrested in May 1918 and was unable to attend the first session of the First Dáil in January 1919. Elected President of the Dáil in his absence, he returned to lead the government when he escaped from prison in February 1919. British insistence on the illegality of the new government led to the War of Independence.

After the truce, de Valera, as President of the Republic, sent a delegation to London to negotiate a treaty. When the resultant treaty was ratified by the Dáil, he resigned over the issue of the Oath of Supremacy, bringing most of the Sinn Féin TDs with him.

The ensuing Civil War between pro- and anti-Treaty forces ended with a ceasefire in May 1923. De Valera was interned. On his release, he decided to take a pragmatic approach to the political impasse, attempting to persuade Sinn Féin to accept the Free State constitution. When this failed, he formed a new party, Fianna Fáil. The party took most of Sinn Féin's seats in the 1927 election, and in the 1932 election it became the largest party in the Dáil, with 72 TDs returned. De Valera was appointed President of the Executive Council. He set about abolishing the requirement for TDs to take the Oath of Supremacy and introduced a new constitution for the Irish State in 1937. He also reneged on loan repayments to Britain, which caused an Economic War with Britain that lasted until 1938.

De Valera's vision of modern Ireland was conservative and Catholic, protecting the 'special position' of the Catholic Church (although the constitution prohibited the establishment of a state religion) and the central role of the family. He refused to relinquish the Republic's claim to the six northern counties. Under his leadership, the Republic remained neutral in World War II, a stance that antagonised Britain and, later, the United States. De Valera was a committed Irish speaker, and Irish was enshrined as the official language of the state, although it was little used in practice.

De Valera remained in the Dáil, either as Taoiseach or in opposition, until 1959, when he was persuaded to run for the office of President of Ireland. He served two terms as President and finally retired in 1973. He died in Dublin on 29 August 1975, aged 92.

William Gladstone 1809–1898

William Ewart Gladstone, the 'Grand Old Man' of British public life, was born in Liverpool on 29 December 1809 into a wealthy merchant family of Scottish descent.

He was educated at Eton College and Oxford University, where he was a keen debater. He became one of the foremost statesmen of the Victorian age, serving four terms as Liberal Prime Minister.

A staunch Christian, Gladstone had originally intended to take holy orders, but he was persuaded by his father to enter politics instead. He was first elected as Member of Parliament to a Conservative seat in Robert Peel's government in 1832. He began to make his mark in junior offices, but was gradually moving towards Liberalism. When the Conservative Party split in 1846, he followed Peel to the Liberal–Conservative offshoot, ultimately joining the Liberal Party in 1859. He was elected leader of the party in 1867 and became Prime Minister in 1868. It was during his four terms as Liberal Prime Minister that he made his mark.

Gladstone introduced major reforms in the spheres of education, justice and the civil service. He also expanded the franchise. One focus of his endeavours was Ireland. In 1869

WILLIAM GLADSTONE

arguing during the Irish Home Rule Bill debate in the House of Commons.

his Irish Church Act disestablished the Protestant Church of Ireland, to which Catholics had previously, unfairly, to pay a tithe. His Land Act of 1870 gave tenants more security of tenure.

After one term as Prime Minister, he lost the 1874 election to the Conservatives, led by his arch-rival, Benjamin Disraeli. In 1880 he began his second term as Prime Minister, but the defeat of the government's budget in 1885, coupled with his failure to rescue General Charles Gordon at Khartoum, dented Gladstone's popularity, and he resigned.

Taking office as Prime Minister for a third time in 1886, he turned his main attention to Ireland. His highly developed Christian moral sense informed everything he did in both the public and private spheres – as an ardent promoter of Balkan and Italian nationalism, he could not, in conscience, continue to deny Ireland the opportunity for increased self-governance. He introduced the first Home Rule Bill in 1886. It passed its first reading in the House of Commons but was defeated on its second reading. The Liberals were defeated in the 1886 election, but Gladstone continued his campaign for Irish home rule while in opposition. He began his fourth and final term as Prime Minister in 1892, and introduced a second Home Rule Bill 1893. This was passed in the Commons, provoking uproar in the unionist camp, but was defeated in the House of Lords.

Gladstone's endeavours had been losing him the support of his own party, and in 1894 he resigned for the last time, to the relief of Queen Victoria, who is said to have found him difficult to work with. He died on 19 May 1898, aged 88, and was buried at Westminster Abbey.

Maud Gonne 1866–1953

Maud Gonne was born into a wealthy family on 21 December 1886 in Surrey, England, near where her father was serving as an officer in the British army.

MAUD GONNE
was an English-born Irish revolutionary, suffragette and actress.

Her mother died of tuberculosis when Maud was still a child; her subsequent childhood was very cosmopolitan, spent travelling with her father and later acting as hostess when he entertained. When her father died in 1886 she became wealthy and embarked on an independent life.

Beautiful and flamboyant, Maud was never short of suitors and had received several marriage proposals by the time she was 18. In Paris she met and fell in love with a married right-wing French nationalist, Lucien Millevoye, with whom she had two children, one of whom died in early childhood. She had also befriended W.B. Yeats, who was smitten by her and proposed to her, famously and unsuccessfully, several times. She was his inspiration for the heroine of the play *Cathleen Ni Houlihan* (1892). Believing that unrequited love inspired his best poetry, she wrote to him that 'the world should thank me for not marrying you'.

As a child, she had spent some time in her father's native Ireland and, despite her cosmopolitan life, formed an attachment to the country and was a supporter of the aspirations of its nationalists. She was deeply affected by an eviction she witnessed in the 1880s and throughout her life had great sympathy for the poor and downtrodden. She was also a cultural nationalist; in 1900 she founded the nationalist group Daughters of Ireland to promote and preserve Irish culture.

She helped to organise the Irish brigades that fought against the British in the Boer War and married an Irish nationalist revolutionary who had fought on the Boer side, Major John MacBride, whom she had met on a fund-raising tour in the United States. The marriage was a stormy one. They separated in 1906, and she was given custody of their only child, Seán, by a French court. MacBride was executed by the British for his part in the 1916 Rising.

In 1918 she was arrested in Dublin for revolutionary activities and imprisoned in England for six months without trial. She became very ill and the authorities released her on condition that she keep out of Ireland. She returned to Ireland immediately and began to campaign on behalf of political prisoners in an effort to improve their conditions.

An early feminist, she regularly spoke on women's rights. She opposed the Treaty and in 1923 she was arrested by Irish Free State forces for seditious activities and imprisoned for 20 days. Later, however, she spoke out against de Valera, who she regarded as having too narrow a view of the future development of the new state.

Honoured by the new republic in 1949 for her efforts during the fight for freedom, she died in Dublin on 27 April 1953.

Arthur Griffith **1871–1922**

Arthur Griffith was born in Dublin on 31 March 1871 into a family of Welsh origin.

ARHTUR GIFFITH
was a journalist and a politician, born in Dublin.

He was one of the main founders of Sinn Féin, acting president of Dáil Éireann in Éamon de Valera's absence in 1919–20, and president of the Dáil from January 1922 until his death in August of the same year.

He worked in the printing industry in Dublin as a typesetter. In 1896 he went to South Africa where he was employed as a miner and journalist and supported the Boers in their cause against the British.

When he returned to Ireland in 1898, he edited several political newspapers and directed his energies to the achievement of home rule through peaceful means. He was in favour of the idea of a dual monarchy, along the lines of that established for Hungary in the Austrian Empire in 1867. He believed that such an approach would be more acceptable to the British than an outright demand for complete independence. The idea never got a foothold in the separatist nationalist thinking of the time.

In 1900 he established Cumann na nGaedheal in an attempt to promote the cause of nationalism through the setting up of small groups and clubs. Around 1903 he gave his organisation the name of a small nationalist newspaper whose press had been seized by the RIC, and Sinn Féin was born, although historians often date the official founding of the party to 1905.

In 1911 he was instrumental in the formation of the Proportional Representation Society of Ireland, believing that PR was a fairer way of voting that would help prevent animosity between republicans and unionists in the united Ireland that he aspired to. It is the voting system still used in the Republic of Ireland – but after partition, Griffith's hypothesis was never put to the test.

A believer in Connolly's nationalism, if not his socialism, Griffith supported the 1916 Rising, although did not participate in it. Despite that, he was picked up after the Rising and was interned in Reading Gaol for eight months. He was jailed on two subsequent occasions for his journalism, which the British regarded as seditious.

It was at his urging that Sinn Féin deputies returned to Westminster in the 1918 general election refused to take their seats in favour of the formation of a national assembly. He opposed Irish participation in World War I and campaigned against the partition of Ireland, a solution put forward by the Ulster Unionists.

Griffith was sent to London by de Valera to head the team of delegates to the Treaty negotiations at the end of the War of Independence. Although the Treaty provided for the partition of Ireland into the 26 southern and six northern counties, Griffith took the pragmatic view that it was the best deal that could be achieved. When it became the catalyst for de Valera's resignation from the Dáil and the outbreak of Civil War, Griffith was elected president of the Dáil. He died in office on 12 August 1922, at the age of 50.

JAMES LARKIN
shown in a
photograph on the
front cover of a
report published by
the *Irish Worker*.

James Larkin 1876–1947

James Larkin was born in Liverpool to Irish parents on 21 January 1876.

When he was five years of age he was sent to Newry, where he was brought up by his grandparents. He went back to Liverpool when he was 12 and found work as a labourer in the docks. A committed Catholic, he soon became a socialist, joining the Independent Labour Party in 1893. His strong Christian beliefs informed his socialism throughout his life.

Larkin became an active union member when he started work as a docker, and in 1906 was elected General Organizer of the National Union of Dock Labourers (NUDL). In 1907 the NUDL sent him to Belfast on a recruitment drive where he recruited 400 new members. After they were sacked, Larkin went to Dublin and recruited 2,700 new members, before forming his own union, the Irish Transport and General Workers' Union (ITGWU). One of the many aims of the union was declared to be 'the land of Ireland for the people of Ireland.' Larkin also established a socialist newspaper, the *Irish Worker*.

1n 1912 Larkin founded the Irish Labour Party with James Connolly. He continued his work with the ITGWU, which had 10,000 members by 1913. Agitation had produced wage increases, but attempts to increase membership led to a lockout of the workers – the 1913 Dublin Lockout. Also with Connolly, Larkin founded the Irish Citizen Army (ICA) to protect striking workers from bullying police tactics. He was arrested for agitation and sentenced to seven months in prison, but protests on his behalf led to his early release. He put all his efforts into raising funds in England and the United States for the striking workers, but the men had to accept the employers' terms or starve when the union finally ran out of money early in 1914.

When World War I started later that year, Larkin encouraged Irishmen not to fight for the British in a conflict that he viewed as one born of capitalist imperialism. He issued an alternative call to arms in the *Irish Worker*: 'Stop at home. Arm for Ireland. Fight for Ireland and no other land.' His Christian beliefs encompassed the idea of a 'just' war against oppression. Meanwhile, James Connolly had expanded the remit of the ICA from self-defence to revolution and the small force was ultimately a key player in the events of the 1916 Rising. Larkin was in America on a speaking tour when it happened. The execution of Connolly in its aftermath was a great personal loss to him.

Imprisoned in New York in 1920 as a result of his communist affiliations, Larkin returned to Ireland on his release in 1923. In 1924 he visited the Soviet Union and afterwards set up a new union, the Irish Workers' Union, the membership of which grew rapidly. He was elected to the Dáil in 1932, although he lost his seat the following year and had to close down the *Irish Worker*. He was re-elected to the Dáil in the next general election. He died in Dublin on 31 January 1947.

David Lloyd George 1863–1945

David George was born in Manchester on 17 January 1893 to Welsh parents.

DAVID LLOYD GEORGE

became British Prime Minister after Herbert Asquith resigned at the end of 1916.

His father died when David was still an infant, and his mother moved the family to Wales, where David's upbringing was supervised by his uncle, a minister who had strong liberal tendencies. He had a great influence on the boy, encouraging him to study hard and to become a lawyer. It was in honour of this uncle that David George added the name 'Lloyd' to his own surname.

On qualifying as a solicitor, he opened his own law practice, but soon moved into politics, entering Westminster as a Liberal MP in 1890. A champion of liberal causes, including land and welfare reform, Lloyd George is remembered in Britain as a reforming politician, responsible for chipping away at the status quo by introducing benefits for workers such as sick pay and unemployment benefits. In effect, he was the founder of the welfare state in Britain.

At the outbreak of World War I, he was Chancellor of the Exchequer, going on to add the munitions ministry to his portfolio, later being given charge of the War Office.

When Prime Minister Herbert Asquith resigned at the end of 1916, the 54-year-old Lloyd George replaced him and presided over the events of the second half of World War I. He was one of the authors of the Versailles Treaty, an undertaking that earned him the Order of Merit.

The Irish question continued to vex Britain and Lloyd George wanted a permanent solution to the problem, which was a drain on Britain's resources. The third Home Rule Bill of 1914 had never come into force (it had been put into abeyance until the end of World War I, a conflict that was generally expected to come to an end at Christmas 1914). The shock of the 1916 Rising and the War of Independence waged by the Irish brought Lloyd George to the realisation that repression was no longer a viable approach in Ireland, and he began the negotiations that would culminate in the setting up of the Irish Free State.

In Ireland, Lloyd George is remembered as the architect of partition, which was enshrined in the Anglo-Irish Treaty with its provision for the six predominantly Protestant and unionist north-eastern counties of Antrim, Armagh, Down, Londonderry, Fermanagh and Tyrone to secede from the Irish Free State within a month of its inception, should they so wish.

In Britain, Lloyd George's political days were numbered; tainted by a scandal surrounding the sale of honours and peerages, and affected by the fallout of a revolt in the Conservative Party, which was governing in coalition with his Liberal Party, he resigned in 1922 and never served in government again. He was leader of the Liberals from 1926 to 1931, but they were out of government and their influence was dwindling. He spent the rest of his days writing his memoirs and died on 26 March 1945.

Constance Markievicz 1868–1927

Constance Gore-Booth was born in London on 4 February 1868 into the Protestant ascendancy.

She was brought up with her sister Eva on the family's estate in Lissadell, County Sligo, where she witnessed her father's philanthropism towards his tenants. W.B. Yeats was a childhood friend and frequent visitor to the estate. When she came of age in 1887, Constance was presented to Queen Victoria. In 1893 she enrolled at the Slade School of Art in London, where she also joined the National Union of Women's Suffrage Societies (NUWSS). While studying in Paris in the late 1890s she met a Polish count, Casimir Dunin Markievicz, and they married in 1900.

In 1903 the couple moved to Dublin, and Constance pursued a career in painting. She was in frequent attendance at Sarah Purser's Dublin salon, where she met nationalist patriots, including Michael Davitt and Maud Gonne. She became interested in revolutionary politics, joining Sinn Féin and the Daughters of Ireland. In 1909 she founded Na Fianna Éireann, a nationalist youth brigade that offered weapons training to boys and girls.

CONSTANCE MARKIEVICZ in the back of a prison van with a nurse after her arrest in Dublin.

Speaking at a meeting in 1911 to protest the visit of King George V to Ireland led to her arrest, but in spite of admitting to attempting to burn the British flag, she was released. In 1913 she joined the ICA and organised food distribution to the striking workers and their families. She paid for the food herself, taking out loans and selling her jewellery. That same year, her husband moved back to his family home in the Ukraine.

In 1916 Markievicz participated in the Rising, fighting at St Stephen's Green. She was arrested, court-martialled and sentenced to death, but the sentence was commuted to life imprisonment. She was released from prison under a general amnesty in 1917, but was imprisoned again in 1918 for plotting against the British government. While in prison, she was elected to the House of Commons, making history as the first female MP. Like the other Sinn Féin MPs, she refused to take her seat at Westminster, taking it instead in the First Dáil in 1919, in which she served as Minister for Labour. She was re-elected to the Second Dáil in 1921. Until 1979 she was the only female cabinet minister in Ireland.

In 1922 Markievicz followed de Valera out of the government in opposition to the Anglo-Irish Treaty and fought on the anti-Treaty side in the Civil War. She wasn't re-elected in the 1922 elections, but was elected for Dublin South in 1923. She joined de Valera's new party, Fianna Fáil, in 1926, and was elected as its candidate for the Fifth Dáil in June 1927, but died before she could take her seat. She had given away all her money and died of complications of appendicitis on 15 July 1927 in a public ward at Sir Patrick Dun's Hospital in Dublin. She was refused a state funeral, and was buried in Glasnevin Cemetery after an oration by Éamon de Valera.

Seán O'Casey 1880–1964

Seán O'Casey was born John Casey in Upper Dorset Street in Dublin's inner city on 30 March 1880.

SEÁN O'CASEY
was an Irish dramatist and memoirist and a committed socialist, writing about the Dublin working classes.

In 1886 his father died and the family fell into poverty. O'Casey taught himself to read and write. He loved drama and theatre and was involved in amateur productions from an early age. He started working at the age of 14.

In 1906 he decided to leave the Protestant Church. He became enthusiastic about Irish nationalism, joining the Gaelic League in 1906, learning to speak Irish and changing his name from John Casey to Seán Ó Cathasaigh. He joined the ITGWU and raised funds for railway workers and their families during the six-month 1913 Dublin Lockout, and it was at this time that began to write purposefully, producing leaflets, pamphlets and ballads, and contributing to the *Irish Worker*.

He joined the ICA and in 1914 he wrote its constitution. However, he became disillusioned with the republican movement because of its emphasis on nationalism rather than socialism and he left the ICA. As a result, he didn't participate in the 1916 Rising.

Soon he was writing plays. *The Shadow of a Gunman*, with its backdrop of nationalist revolution, was first performed in the Abbey Theatre in 1923. *Juno and the Paycock* followed in 1924 and *The Plough and the Stars* in 1926. This third play caused riots in the theatre – the audience thought it was an attack on the heroes of the 1916 Rising. Notoriety made the play popular and O'Casey's earning power increased to the extent that he was able to devote himself completely to writing. His 1946 play *Red Roses for Me* was set during the Dublin Lockout in 1913.

In 1926 he was awarded the Hawthornden Prize for *Juno and the Paycock*. He travelled to England to receive the award and met the actress Eileen Reynolds Carey. They married in 1927 and had three children.

His next play, the anti-war, anti-imperialist *The Silver Tassie*, was rejected by the Abbey in 1928, and O'Casey was so bitter he decided not to return to Dublin. The play and its rejection became something of a *cause célèbre* when O'Casey sent the Abbey correspondence to the London newspapers and *The Silver Tassie* was staged in London the following year.

O'Casey's later plays were well received and frequently performed, but it is his first three, the Dublin Trilogy of *The Shadow of a Gunman*, *Juno and the Paycock* and *The Plough and the Stars*, whose popularity has endured.

In the 1930s O'Casey lectured at universities in Britain and America and was an enthusiastic writer of letters to newspapers. He wrote a huge autobiography and a series of articles about the theatre. He became entrenched in his socialist beliefs during the fascist era, and he was blacklisted as a 'dangerous subversive' during America's McCarthy era. In response to Catholic Church censorship of the arts, he banned further productions of his work in Ireland.

On 18 September 1964 he died following a heart attack and was cremated in England.

DANIEL O'CONNELL
spent much of his
early life with his
uncle at Derrynane
House near Waterville,
County Kerry.

Daniel O'Connell 1775–1847

Daniel O'Connell, the 'Liberator', was born in Caherciveen, County Kerry, on 6 August 1775.

He was adopted by a wealthy childless uncle and received a good education. He studied law in London and was called to the Irish bar on 19 May 1798.

The anti-Catholic Penal Laws, enacted from the late 17th century, had gradually eroded the position of Catholics under the law. On 23 May 1798 the United Irishmen staged a rebellion, which was violently suppressed by the government forces. O'Connell did not condone violence and did not support that rebellion, or Robert Emmett's rebellion of 1803, believing that change could only come through political means. However, as a barrister, he was always ready to defend those accused of political crimes, and he performed his role ably and with passion.

In 1811 O'Connell founded the Catholic Board to campaign for Catholic emancipation (that is, the right for Catholics to run for parliament). In 1823 he established the Catholic Association, which campaigned for broader change, in areas such as tenants' rights and economic development. The annual subscription of a shilling was used to fund the campaign for Catholic emancipation.

As a result of the campaign, the official British line began to soften after several years, so O'Connell decided the time was right to take things a step further. In 1828 he stood as parliamentary candidate in a by-election in County Clare. He won the election, but was unable to take his seat because the Oath of Supremacy instituted by Henry VIII required all MPs to swear allegiance to the king as Supreme Governor of the Church of England and this was incompatible with Catholicism. The Duke of Wellington and Sir Robert Peel, Prime Minister and Home Secretary respectively, could see that preventing O'Connell taking his seat would lead to more unrest and violence in Ireland, so they worked to establish the right of all Christians to sit in Parliament and the right became law in 1829. However, it was not applied retrospectively and O'Connell had to win another election in order to take his seat in February 1830.

Having achieved Catholic emancipation, O'Connell turned his efforts to the repeal of the Act of Union, which had been passed in 1801 to establish the United Kingdom of Great Britain and Ireland. O'Connell's Repeal Association wanted the two kingdoms to separate, with Queen Victoria to be queen of Ireland, but his tactic of holding 'monster meetings' to promote repeal led to his being convicted of conspiracy. He served three months in prison. Without his leadership, the Repeal Association began to splinter.

O'Connell went on a pilgrimage to Rome in 1847, but his health had suffered during his time in prison and the cold weather on the trip weakened him still further. He died in Genoa on 15 May 1847. His heart is buried in Rome in the Irish College chapel and his body in a mausoleum in Glasnevin cemetery.

Daniel O'Connell is revered as one of Ireland's greatest statesmen and the country abounds in memorials to him, not least of which is Dublin's main thoroughfare, formerly Sackville Street, renamed O'Connell Street in his honour.

Charles Stewart Parnell 1846–1891

Charles Stewart Parnell was born into a wealthy Anglo-Irish family in Avondale in County Wicklow in 1846.

He is best remembered for his tireless work as a campaigner for Irish home rule in the late 19th century.

He supported the idea of self-government for Ireland, and after unsuccessfully standing for Parliament as a Home Rule League candidate on two occasions, he was finally elected as MP for Meath in 1875. He quickly earned the respect of his peers. In 1879 he was elected president of the newly established National Land League. When the famine and subsequent economic depression left many rural tenants without the means to pay their rent, Parnell travelled the country, exhorting them to stand up to their landlords and to refuse to allow themselves to be dispossessed.

CHARLES STEWART PARNELL
addressing a meeting.

In 1880 he became leader of the Irish Parliamentary Party. The 1885 election resulted in a hung parliament, with the majority of seats going to the Liberals, but giving the balance of parliamentary power to the 86 Irish Parliamentary Party MPs. At first they supported the Conservatives, but a change of policy caused Parnell to switch allegiance. The Conservative government fell and the Liberals were returned to power in early 1886.

The Liberal Prime Minister, William Gladstone, backed the idea of home rule and introduced the first Irish Home Rule Bill in April of that year. The bill was contentious, the Liberals being deeply divided on the issue, and it was narrowly defeated on its second reading. The government fell, and the new elections produced a Conservative government supported by a group of breakaway Liberal MPs. It was the death knell for Parnell's home rule ambitions.

In 1887 *The Times* published a forged letter that suggested Parnell had supported the murders of Lord Frederick Cavendish and Thomas Henry Burke, the Irish Chief Secretary and Under-Secretary, in the Phoenix Park in Dublin. However, a commission of enquiry cleared him and he successfully sued *The Times*.

Having survived the scandal, in 1889 Parnell was named as co-respondent in a divorce between Captain William O'Shea and his wife Katharine (Kitty), with whom Parnell had been conducting a long-standing relationship – they had three children together. Parnell decided not to appear in court and the divorce was granted, leaving the way clear for him to marry Kitty on 25 June 1891. However, even though the O'Sheas had already separated before the liaison began, such was the moral sensibility of the times that Parnell was forever tainted. The Kitty O'Shea affair provoked a split in the Irish Parliamentary Party and eventually brought about Parnell's resignation from the parliamentary party.

He continued to campaign tirelessly for home rule, but events had taken their toll on his health and he died at his home in Hove, East Sussex, on 6 October 1891, just a few months after his marriage. One of Ireland's greatest statesmen, the 'Blackbird of Avondale' is commemorated in Dublin with the naming of Parnell Street and Parnell Square and with a monument at the north end of O'Connell Street, inscribed with an extract from one of his speeches: 'No man has the right to set a boundary to the onward march of a nation'.

KITTY O'SHEA
in 1879.

Pádraig Pearse **1879–1916**

Pádraig Pearse was born in Dublin on 10 November 1879.

His father was an English stonemason and his mother had moved to Dublin from County Meath during the famine years.

During his schooldays Pearse developed an interest in Irish history, culture and language. He studied law and was called to the bar at King's Inns in Dublin in 1901, the same year in which he embarked on a degree course in modern languages. His interest in Irish grew and he became a director of the Gaelic League, which had been founded in 1893 to promote and protect the native language. From 1903 to 1909 he edited the league's newspaper, *An Claidheamh Soluis*. He also wrote poetry in Irish and collected tales and fables from old manuscripts. His vision of a free Ireland was a romantic one. He promoted the teaching of Irish history and culture in schools and in 1908 he founded St Enda's School, Scoil Éanna, in Ranelagh, a bilingual school that taught these subjects.

Pearse came to politics as a result of his love for Irish culture. When the Irish Volunteers were formed in 1913 Pearse became a member of their provisional committee and a contributor to their publication, *The Irish Volunteer*.

PÁDRAIG PEARSE played an active role in the preparations for the 1916 Rising.

In 1914 he was co-opted to the Supreme Council of the IRB. Shortly afterwards, the Irish Volunteers split, and Pearse aligned himself with the more extreme nationalist faction, opposing Irish support for Britain in the war in Europe. He became convinced that the only way that Ireland would win its freedom from the oppressive yoke of Britain was through a blood sacrifice. He wanted complete independence – the limited home rule offered by the third Home Rule Bill, suspended for the duration of the war, was no longer enough. He was a rousing public speaker, and his oration at the funeral of Sinn Féin veteran Jeremiah O'Donovan Rossa in August 1915 made his position clear.

In the early months of 1915, Pearse began planning the 1916 Rising in his capacity as a Military Council member of the IRB. When the Rising started, he expected the citizens of Dublin to come out in support of the rebels. Even though they failed to do this, and with the Rising clearly failing, he read the Proclamation of the Irish Republic from the steps of the GPO. Anticipating his own death, he prophesied:

'When we are all wiped out, people will blame us for everything … in a few years they will see the meaning of what we tried to do.'

He surrendered to the British forces on 28 April, was tried by court martial for treason and was sentenced to death. He was executed on 3 May 1916. A member of the execution party reported that he whistled on the way to his execution. Pearse achieved his real fame in death. He is usually the first person that people think of in connection with the Rising that was the catalyst for the independence of the nation.

John Redmond 1856–1918

John Redmond was born in County Wexford on 1 September 1856.

JOHN REDMOND
was opposed to the use of physical force. He was educated at Trinity College, Dublin.

The Redmonds were an old Wexford family of Anglo-Norman stock. Redmond's mother came from a Protestant unionist family; she converted to Catholicism, but not to nationalism, on her marriage.

Redmond's reputation for seriousness was established early in his life. He was educated at the Jesuit Clongowes Wood College and studied law at Trinity College, Dublin, but left in 1876 before taking his degree. He went to live in London with his father, who was unwell, and became interested in politics. He worked as clerk in the House of Commons and was impressed by the Irish drive towards self-government and particularly by Charles Stewart Parnell, to whom he remained loyal until the statesman's death.

Redmond began attending political meetings with Parnell in 1879. He stood for election in New Ross, Wexford, in 1881 and won the seat. He went on fund-raising trips to the United States and Australia between 1883 and 1884, collecting donations to further the cause of home rule. When the Irish Parliamentary Party split in 1890, Redmond was elected leader of the smaller Parnellite faction. He ran for election in Waterford in 1891 and retained the seat until his death.

Home rule for Ireland was Redmond's aim, but the Liberal Party was lukewarm in its response to his lobbying. After the 1910 elections, however, the Liberals needed the support of Redmond's party to maintain the balance of power. This worked to the advantage of Redmond and the Irish cause, and he took the opportunity to engineer the introduction of the third Home Rule Bill. This was opposed by the Ulster Unionists, who were given the option to secede in the Home Rule Act, passed in the House of Commons in 1914. It all became academic when Britian entered the war in Europe, and the bill was put on the back burner until the end of the conflict. Redmond supported the Allied cause and was confident that after a short but bloody conflict in Europe the war would end and Ireland would, finally, have home rule.

Achieving independence through violent means was never part of Redmond's credo – he was a parliamentarian through and through. However, by 1916 Irish patience had run out and the Rising that erupted in Easter of that year destroyed Redmond's hopes for home rule as a solution. In July 1916, David Lloyd George was sent to Ireland to negotiate a new home rule bill, giving in to unionist demands for a reduction in Irish representation at Westminister. Redmond accused the British government of treachery, but agreed to participate in a convention to settle the matter of home rule for Ireland. He almost achieved his aim of an all-Ireland home rule, but was defeated at the eleventh hour. Disappointed and ill, he withdrew his motion and resigned.

Redmond died after surgery for an intestinal blockage on 6 March 1918. He was given the sacrament of the sick by a Jesuit priest who reported that one of the last things he said was, 'Father, I am a broken-hearted man.'

William Butler (W.B.) Yeats 1865–1939

William Butler Yeats was born on 13 June 1865 in Sandymount, County Dublin.

W.B. YEATS
was an Irish poet and one of the foremost literary figures in the 20th century.

Descended from the Anglo-Norman Butlers of Ormond, the family belonged to the Protestant ascendancy. His painter father always had difficulty making ends meet.

The family moved to London when William was still a toddler, and he spent the next 14 years there. Educated at home for several years, he didn't shine at school when he eventually attended one. In 1880 the family returned to Dublin and William studied at the Metropolitan School of Art from 1884 to 1886. It was at this time he began writing poetry. His first works were published in *The Dublin University Review* in 1885.

The family went back to London in 1887, and in 1890 Yeats joined the Hermetic Order of the Golden Dawn, a secret society that dabbled in the occult. He also co-founded the Rhymers' Club – rhythm and cadence were always important to Yeats.

Yeats' interest in the theatre had been encouraged by his father and in 1904 Dublin's Abbey Theatre was opened as a national theatre, with Yeats as one of its three directors.

In 1889 Yeats met Maud Gonne and fell passionately in love with her. He proposed to her four times. He was very upset when she married the Irish nationalist John MacBride. Initially, Yeats had no sympathy for the nationalist cause, but he changed his mind after the 1916 Rising, in the aftermath of which MacBride was one of those executed. Some of Yeats's most beautiful and haunting poetry was written after the Rising, in acknowledgement of the sacrifice made by those who had instigated it and paid the ultimate price.

In 1917 Yeats married 25-year-old Georgiana Hyde-Lees and they had a daughter and a son, Anne and Michael. The couple shared an interest in the occult. The spirit communications they received during séances were recounted by Yeats in *A Vision* (1925). The importance of the occult in Yeats's life is manifest in his own claim that this was his 'book of books'.

Yeats had backed the government side in the Civil War and in 1922 was appointed to the Irish upper house, Seanad Éireann. He accepted the appointment, although the violence of the war lingered on, putting government members at risk of attack and assassination. He was a fierce opponent of the bond between the new state and the Catholic Church, believing it to be an insurmountable obstacle to the eventual inclusion of Northern Ireland in the Republic. He retired from the Senate in 1928 owing to poor health.

In 1923 Yeats was awarded the Nobel Prize for Literature for his poetry, an accolade that he received as an honour for the new state. Sales of his books rocketed and Yeats had money for the first time in his life.

Yeats died at Menton in France on 28 January 1939. In 1948 his remains were moved to Drumcliff in County Sligo, where they were re-interred.

List of illustrations and picture credits

p3 Photograph by W.J. Westropp, May 1916 By permission of the Royal Irish Academy. © RIA

p7 Photograph by W.J. Westropp, May 1916 By permission of the Royal Irish Academy. © RIA

p9 Scene at the GPO, painting by Norman Teeling

p11 Silk cigarette card, private collection, Teapot Press

p13 Engraving, private collection, Teapot Press

p14 Oil on canvas portrait of *Henry Grattan (1746–1820)* by Martin Archer Shee (1769–1850) National Gallery of Ireland

p15 *Charles Cornwallis, 1st Marquess Cornwallis* by Thomas Gainsborough, oil on canvas, feigned oval, 1783, National Portrait Gallery, London

p16 Domer48 at English Wikipedia

p17 Engraving, private collection, Teapot Press

pp18-19 Print by J. Kirwan, Library of Congress

p20 Rodrigo Garrido/ Shutterstock

p21 Engraving, private collection, Teapot Press

p22 Engraving, private collection, Teapot Press

p24 Illustration, Teapot Press

p25 Illustration, Teapot Press

p26 Vincent MacNamara / Shutterstock

p26 Illustration, Teapot Press

p27 Illustration, Teapot Press

p29 Illustration, Teapot Press

p30 Illustration, Teapot Press

p31 Print, Library of Congress

p31 Illustration, Teapot Press

p32 Creative Commons

p33 Illustration, Teapot Press

p34 Tupungato / Shutterstock

p35 Illustration, Teapot Press

p36 Illustration, Teapot Press

p37 Cigarette card, private collection

p38 *The Graphic*, 1916, Teapot Press

p39 Stamp, Raven Stamps Ltd, ravenstamps.com

p39 Illustration, Teapot Press

p39 National Library of Ireland

p40 Illustration, Teapot Press

p41 Print, private collection, Teapot Press

p42 Illustration, Teapot Press

p43 Illustration, Teapot Press

p44 Illustration, Teapot Press

p45 *The Graphic*, 1916, Teapot Press

p47 National Library of Ireland

p48 *James Connolly and the Citizen Army, Dublin* (Executed 1916), Harry Kernoff, 20th century, National Gallery of Ireland

p49 Villanova University, open source

p50 Wikipedia

p51 Photograph, Library of Congress

p52 Villanova University, open source

p53 National Portrait Gallery, London

p54 Photograph, Wikimedia

p55 National Library of Ireland

p56 Osioni, Wikimedia

p57 Library of Congress, Printer: Hely's Limited, Restoration: Adam Cuerden

p58 Wikimedia Creative Commons

p59 Wikimedia Creative Commons

p60 Wikimedia Creative Commons

p61 National Library of Ireland

p62 Postcard, Private collection

p63 *Leitrim Observer*

p65 Illustration, Teapot Press

p66 Illustration, Teapot Press

p67 Illustration, Teapot Press

p68 *Portrait of Roger Casement*, Sarah Henrietta Purser, 1848-1943, National Gallery of Ireland

p69 Illustration, Teapot Press

p71 Illustration, Teapot Press

p72 *Vanity Fair*, 1906

p73 Wikimedia Creative Commons

p74 Villanova University, open source

p75 *Men of the West*, (detail) Sean Keating, © DACS, Hugh Lane Gallery

p77 Illustration, Bob Moulder, Teapot Press

p78 The National Archives of Ireland

p79 *Le Miroir*, 1916, Teapot Press

p80 Illustration, Teapot Press

p81 Illustration, Teapot Press

pp82-83 Illustration, Bob Moulder, Teapot Press